Anthea Simmons

Burning Sunlight

Annotations by Sabrina Dowie

Ernst Klett Sprachen
Stuttgart

Bildquellennachweis
4 (c) Anthea Simmons; **216** Shutterstock (HowLettery), New York

1. Auflage   1 ⁶ ⁵ ⁴ ³ ² | 2027 26 25 24 23

Worterklärungen von Sabrina Dowie

Redaktion: Astrid Proctor
Gestaltung und Satz: Joachim Schrimm, ETYPO, Friolzheim
Umschlaggestaltung: Andersen Press, London (Design by Jack Noel);
Eva Lettenmayer
Titelbild: Andersen Press, London; Getty Images (Victoria Gnatiuk), München;
Shutterstock (Ollyy), New York; Getty Images (AntonioGuillem)
Druck und Bindung: Plump Druck & Medien GmbH, Rheinbreitbach

Printed in Germany
ISBN 978-3-12-542652-8

Contents

Abbreviations used in the annotations

abbr of	abbreviation of	*sb*	somebody
dial	dialect	*sing*	singular
idm	idiom	*sl*	slang (be careful how you use it)
inf	informal		
off	offensive	*sth*	something
opp of	opposite of	*usu*	usually
pl	plural	*vulg*	vulgar

About the author

© Anthea Simmons

Anthea Simmons lives in Devon with her polydactyl cat, Caramac. After a successful career in the City of London and working for a while as a teacher, her son Henry finally persuaded her to start writing. She is the author of *Share, The Best Best Baby, I'm Big Now* 5 and *Lightning Mary* and *Burning Sunlight*. She campaigns for European values and a fairer democracy.

1 **polydactyl** having more than the usual number of toes on its paws

About Klett Augmented

We have added some extra materials to this book which you can access with the Klett-Augmented-App:

- A **vocabulary training tool** containing words and phrases that will be helpful when you talk and write about the topics and themes of this story (scan page 216).
- An **online quiz** that will help you check how well you have understood what happens in the story (e.g. page 25).

To access this material, install the Klett-Augmented-App on your mobile device, choose "Burning Sunlight" from the list and then scan the pages with the Augmented Icon on them: ⌐⊞⊞⌐

| Klett-Augmented-App kostenlos downloaden und öffnen | Seite mit diesem Symbol scannen | Medien laden, direkt nutzen oder speichern |

Apple und das Apple-Logo sind Marken der Apple Inc., die in den USA und weiteren Ländern eingetragen sind. App Store ist eine Dienstleistungsmarke der Apple Inc. | Google Play und das Google Play-Logo sind Marken der Google Inc.

To Alex, who read as I wrote, critiqued brilliantly and rescued many iterations of the manuscripts lost through my tech ineptitude, saving me from total meltdown!

*And to Henry, as ever.
Precious beyond words.*

LUCAS

I lay on the smooth marble floor of the Natural History Museum, staring up through the bones of the giant 3D model of the ichthyosaur. It was as extinct as humankind would be if we didn't do something soon. I was playing dead, but my heart was beating
5 as fast as a hummingbird's wings.

Around me, a sea of bodies covered in sheets, with only their whitened faces visible. Eyes closed. Barely breathing.

There was an eerie silence. It made me think of the stillness and quiet on the moors before a storm blew in. Only we were the storm,
10 this time.

I felt fear and elation as we waited, waited, waited. Surely people could hear my heart, which thumped wildly underneath the bag of paint taped to my chest?

Zaynab lay next to me, her bony elbow sticking into my side, her
15 crutch propped against my leg.

'You won't chicken out, will you?' she hissed under her breath. 'Promise! Promise me you are in!'

I turned my head towards her. She had asked me this a million times. Nothing had changed. She fixed me with her fierce stare and
20 my heart stopped for a moment.

'Well?'

I nodded.

'I'm in. I promise.'

She moved her elbow just enough to stop my ribs hurting. We
25 closed our eyes and got back to the die-in.

In a few minutes, we'd die again and wake the world up.

Oh yes.

---

2 **bone** one of the hard pieces that make the structure inside a person – 3 **extinct** no longer existing – 5 **hummingbird** *Kolibri* – 11 **elation** very great happiness – 15 **crutch** *Krücke* – 16 **to chicken out** *(idm, inf)* decide not to do sth because your are too nervous – 19 **fierce** *here:* very intense – 25 **die-in** form of protest where sb simulates being dead

ZAYNAB

I did not want to go to the UK, even if it was where Mama was born and I lived until I was four. I did not want to leave Mama. I didn't want to go somewhere I would no longer see her everywhere I looked, or hear her voice, or even almost feel her touch, and I did
5 not understand why Father would want to, either.

Except, I was forgetting. For him, his work came first, before everything – even Mama with cancer. Even Mama gone and me on my own, missing her so badly that I could barely see the point of going on.

10 And now his work was tearing me out of the place where Mama and I had laid our roots, except that Mama remained deep in Somaliland soil, buried beneath one of the yeheb bushes which she had helped so many people to plant in the fight against the endless droughts.

15 'The change will be good for us. It will help us to forget,' Father said, as we were driven to the airport.

I said nothing in return. It seemed to me that he had already forgotten. Mama would have hated this trip. She would have hated that we were flying, hated that we were abandoning people who
20 needed our help and turning our backs on the work she had done with the rest of the team at the charity to keep women safe in camps, to plant trees, to help them find a way to make a living when they had lost everything to the desert as it spread, destroying their farms.

'And it'll be an adventure. Something for you to tell your friends
25 about!' he added. He had completely failed to notice that I had stopped hanging out with my friends since Mama died, that they bored me with their silly talk, that I was truly alone.

---

7 **cancer** *Krebs* – 12 **yeheb bush** plant that grows in the deserts of Somaliland –
14 **drought** [draʊt] long period when it does not rain – 19 **to abandon** to leave behind

We spent the first night in the UK in a hotel near Heathrow. We'd been travelling for thirteen hours including the stop in Dubai. We were tired and it was cold. Not that it didn't get cold in Borama. It did. This was a different cold. I began to shiver and felt as if the shivering would never stop. I stood in the hotel room with its dim light and huge bed and white, shiny bathroom and stared at the tray of sandwiches which had no flavour, and I knew I was shivering with hatred and sadness. People said I was lucky to have this opportunity. I did not feel lucky. I was being torn away from my home and from Mama and everything that reminded me of her. I dug around in my suitcase and brought out a scarf that had been hers. It still smelled of her perfume and I buried my face in the fabric and breathed deeply, then I set it aside and fished out my phone. I had downloaded an app to allow me to find Mecca. The qibla appeared on my screen, flickered and swung, settling in the direction of the door. I unrolled my mat and began my evening prayers. The focus cleared my mind of anger, but the inner calm did not last long.

I could hear my father in the next-door room, taking a shower. I began counting the minutes. One. Two. Three. Four. Five. Six.

I felt anger growing inside me, spreading like a poison.

Ten. Eleven.

Finally, the noise of the shower stopped.

There is a saying in my religion: *The believer is not the one who eats his fill when the neighbour beside him is hungry.* It should also have said *'or wastes water when others go thirsty'.*

I waited for a moment or two and then I hammered on the wall and shouted: 'You hypocrite! You total hypocrite!'

Nothing.

Five minutes later, a knock at my door.

I ignored it, got into the bed with all my clothes on and fell asleep, with Mama's scarf held close.

4 **to shiver** to shake with cold – 15 **qibla** direction of the sacred mosque in Mecca, which is used by Muslims when they pray – 21 **poison** *Gift* – 28 **hypocrite** ['hɪpəkrɪt] *Heuchler(in)*

ZAYNAB

My father was looking out the window of the train, pointing at things, trying to get me to pay attention, describing what he was seeing in a loud voice. I could hear him above the music in my headphones.

'Look at the rich soil in those ploughed fields. What fat sheep and
5   cattle! See how lush that grass is, even now, after summer. They have none of our problems.'

He was trying to sell this place to me. Yeah. It was all green. Yeah. The cows and sheep were fat instead of scrawny. Did I really need to be told that this country was lucky?

10   A bit of me wanted to look out of the window, too, but then he'd have won. I closed my eyes and turned up the volume and soon I was asleep.

I dreamed I was back home. The grey hills and mountains in the distance. The turquoise and red roofs. The brightly-coloured domes
15   of the nomads' aqals. The gob trees' twisted trunks and birds' nests of thorny branches.

And then my mother was there, too, braiding my hair, telling me about the latest family she had helped, the little girl she had fed, the woman she had taught to read. Only now she really was not
20   with me. In my sleep, I could feel the tears coming. I could feel that I was half in the past, half in the present and I felt like I really wanted to stay in the past with Mama.

When Father woke me, a cry came out of me so loud that the other passengers all stared at me in horror and shock. My father
25   felt he had to apologise to them. They looked away, embarrassed.

'You were dreaming,' he said, trying to take my hand. I pulled it away and he sat back in his seat and pointed out of the window, again.

---

4 **to plough** [plaʊ] *pflügen* – 15 **aqal** temporary hut used by Somali nomads – 15 **trunk** thick stem of a tree

'I was dreaming of Mama,' I said, searching his face for signs that he understood, but he just looked excited, like a child.

'I had to wake you to see this. Look!'

On one side, there was nothing but grey sea, heaving backwards and forwards like water in a bucket. The clouds seemed to skim the surface. It looked cold and unwelcoming. Through the other window, dark, ugly red rock rose up high. It must have been crumbling because there was wire netting all over it to trap any falling stones.

The train seemed to be travelling on a tightrope between the land and the sea.

'Just like home, eh?'

No. Not at all. It was nothing like the warm, orangey red of our soil. This was a dirty, dark red, like dried blood.

He didn't wait for my answer but went on, talking like he was a guidebook or something. 'This railway line has been washed away many times,' he told me, proudly. 'We are lucky there have been no severe storms this year. The railway is at risk from climate change and when the sea levels rise or the storms damage the rails and the line fails, it hits this region hard. Trade and tourism both suffer.'

'How sad for them,' I said, looking out to the sea, which had merged with the sky in one great, grey lump.

He frowned. 'I am just saying that we are all, in our different ways, in the same boat ... or on the same train!'

He laughed at his own pathetic joke. Perhaps he was beginning to realise that he had made a mistake, coming back to this cold country with its privileged problems. It was a bit late for that.

'And that rock is nothing like ours,' I added and closed my eyes again. Even with them closed, I could almost see him, looking at me, searching my face for some love, some respect. Bit late for that, too.

Ten minutes later, he was reaching for my hand again.

---

6 **surface** the top part of sth – 18 **severe** serious, terrible – 22 **to merge** to combine or join to become one – 25 **pathetic** *jämmerlich*

'Come. We have arrived. This is our station.'

We heaved our bags out of the train and onto the platform. It was raining and beginning to get dark. I still felt as if I had left part of myself in my dream and that I was now in a sort of nightmare. People were staring at us. I pulled my hijab further over my head to hide as much of my face as possible and stumbled after Father, through the ticket barrier and out onto the street. It all looked so cold. So grey. So dead.

We stood together for a while, feeling the rain soak into our clothes. I began to shiver again. Father pulled me close but I held myself away from him, stiffly, and after a moment he let go.

Someone tut-tutted and said, irritably, 'Should have stood over there, under the canopy.'

The woman who had spoken stood in front of us. Big. Wearing a massive woolly jumper covered in some disgusting crusty stains and what looked like clumps of animal fur. She smelled of cigarettes and something that reminded me of wet camel. I felt a pang of homesickness again.

'You the professor?' she asked, in the same aggressive tone.

'I am!' Father switched on his most powerful smile, teeth gleaming, eyes wide. She stared at him for a moment and then at me, before grabbing my suitcase and heading off for a car left with the engine running and the boot open. Father followed her, dragging his case, which she hoisted in as if it were as light as a feather.

The car had *Bea's Cabs* down the side and stickers of bees all over it. Was it a joke or couldn't she spell?

'Well, get in!' she said, impatiently.

The car smelled worse than she did, mainly because of various plastic trees hanging from drawing pins in the roof, which stank of something sweet and fake.

'Just you two, then?' she said, swinging the car out in front of a bus and then making a U-turn before putting her foot down.

---

7 **ticket barrier** *Sperre (zur Fahrkartenkontrolle)* – 12 **to tut-tut** to make a sound that expresses disapproval or irritation – 13 **canopy** *Vordach* – 15 **stain** dirty mark – 16 **fur** *Fell, Tierhaare* – 24 **to hoist** to lift

'Just we two.'

'Where's your wife to, then? Left her behind, have you?'

'Yes. We have left her behind.' My father turned his head to look out of the car window but not before I had time to raise my eyebrows
5 in a silent question.

'Probably for the best. Bloody awful weather here, pardon my French. What are you a professor of, then?'

'Economics, but I am here as part of a project on climate change and environmental sustainability.' My father said it in such a way
10 that any normal person would have realised that he did not want to talk and so would shut up but not this Bea/Bee woman.

She laughed and laughed, hitting the steering wheel with the flat of her hand and rocking backwards and forwards in her seat. 'You've had a change of climate right enough!'
15 She thought she was funny.

We sat in silence. Nothing to look at as darkness fell. The road twisted and turned up and down hills. I felt sick. The smell. The twisting. The homesickness.

She caught my eye in her mirror.
20 'Don't you dare be sick in my cab, young lady! Five minutes tops. Shut your mouth and hold it in.'

She was accelerating hard as she spoke, and as we rounded a sharp corner at a crazy speed, I suddenly saw a figure in the road – a boy, his face white in the cab headlights.
25 He looked just like a ghost. Or just about to be made one.

I think I screamed.

---

6 **pardon my French** *(idm, inf)* to say sorry for using a word that might be offensive –
8 **economics** *(sing)* finance and commerce – 9 **sustainability** *Nachhaltigkeit* – 20 **cab**
taxi – 20 **tops** *(inf)* at the most – 22 **to accelerate** [ək'seləreɪt] to go faster and faster

LUCAS

Saturdays were good days for me. Everyone was out. Dad was with his mate, Stu, fishing. Mum was working in the supermarket in Yewburton, the little town where I went to school, three miles down the road from our hamlet. Lara, my seventeen-year-old sister, was
5 in her room on her phone or out with her mates from college – shopping, usually. By lunchtime, I'd have done the washing-up and hung out the laundry.

Dad said I should get a Saturday job. He said that's what he did and that's how he got a bike and a proper football and all that sort
10 of thing. It would've been good to earn some money, but there were no Saturday jobs for young kids. So, there you go, end of that idea.

Dad took me fishing once, but I hated it. He and Stu just smoked rollies (which I had to make for them) and talked about stories in the papers and how everything was a disgrace or a shambles. I didn't
15 join in. I couldn't. They laughed at things that I did not think were funny at all. Plus I felt very sorry for the fish, struggling to get away and then gasping for air while Dad and Stu took photos of each other holding them. They did put them back in the water, but I think there was one that didn't make it. Dad let go of it too quickly, Stu
20 said. It just rolled over and sank.

I didn't think I was ever really going to get on with my dad.

As I remembered that horrible morning, a thought just hit me. I wasn't ever, EVER going to get on with my dad. We had nothing in common.

25 That was part of the reason I liked Saturdays. No Dad.

Some people cannot be on their own. There were people in my class who would've gone nuts if they hadn't got anyone to talk to, and who jabbered all the time and usually just rubbish. I was not like them. I preferred being on my own. I liked silence.

4 **hamlet** a very small village – 14 **shambles** *(pl, inf)* chaos, total disorder – 16 **to struggle** to fight – 21 **to get on with sb** to have a good relationship with sb – 27 **to go nuts** *(idm, inf)* to go crazy

Mostly, I went up on the moors. I didn't care whether it was raining (which it usually was) or sunny. Best of all was when I could see a storm coming in from the sea, miles away, heading for the moors like a massive army of black and grey fighters. I'd sit on one

5 of the huge rocks that lie around as if they've been tossed by giants and wait for the clouds to arrive and throw down rain that hit me as hard as a million javelins or arrows and got through my clothes so that I was soaked to the skin. I'd get really cold but I also felt kind of wild, like I was part of the land and we were being attacked

10 together and I might even dissolve into the moss and the lichen, and soak in like blood. Maybe that meant I was a bit weird. I don't know. I just felt like I belonged there.

I tried to sketch the moor, but it was hard to capture just how alien it is – like another planet. The stars were so clear and seemed

15 so close that you could believe you were in a whole different dimension. I wanted to capture the colour changes when clouds passed over or the sun broke through, and also the cattle, Belted Galloways, who were scattered across the brown and yellow and green like dominos, with their white bands round their tummies

20 standing out against their thick, black coats. I loved these 'Belties' who roam about, grazing wherever they want and sometimes stand in the road, in front of a tourist's car usually, refusing to move.

When I was on my own, thinking or dreaming of a painting I might make one day, I just wandered about all over the place, a bit

25 like a Beltie on the moors, not planning my route, getting soaked, feeling stubborn for no reason. And that's how I felt that day, sitting on a rock, just watching the weather rolling and swirling and changing all around and trying to ignore the fact that night was creeping across the sky and it would soon be impossibly dark on

30 the lane back home. And I'd forgotten my torch.

---

5 **to toss** to throw – 7 **javelin** a long spear – 7 **arrow** long thin weapon that is shot from a bow *(Pfeil)* – 8 **soaked** very wet – 10 **to dissolve** to melt, to mix with – 10 **lichen** ['laɪkən] *Flechte* – 13 **to capture** *here:* to draw it perfectly – 17 **cattle** cows and bulls – 18 **to scatter** to spread – 20 **coat** fur or hair of an animal – 21 **to roam** to wander, to walk with no fixed direction – 26 **stubborn** unwilling to change one's mind – 29 **to creep** to move quietly and slowly

When I started off down the hill, I let myself get into a sort of rhythm, letting the hill and gravity pull me forwards and down. I couldn't see much. The trees that line the lane shut out the last of the sun and the blackness started to be almost thick enough to
5 touch. All I could hear was the rain and the slap of my feet on the Tarmac. I felt hypnotised, almost, so when Bea's cab came screaming round the corner, I very nearly just stayed in the road for her to run me over. Instead, some instinct made me jump in the hedge while Bea's brakes squealed madly as she swerved to miss me.

10 I must have given her a scare because she was super angry when she wound down the window. She had passengers in the back. I couldn't really make them out but it looked like a man and a kid, maybe about my age.

Bea had a good old rant about wearing dark clothes and not
15 having a torch and what the hell did I think I was doing ambling along in the middle of the road. Going to tell my dad. Blah, blah, blah.

I said I was sorry and she wound up the window and roared off, leaving a stinking diesel cloud behind her.

20 I could have been killed, but I wasn't. That's life.

---

2 **gravity** *Schwerkraft* – 6 **Tarmac** *Asphalt* – 8 **instead** alternatively – 8 **hedge** row of bushes or small trees – 9 **to squeal** to make a high-pitched sound, to shriek – 14 **rant** speaking in a loud way – 15 **to amble** to stroll, to walk slowly

ZAYNAB

'Bloody idiot! Could have killed him! Bloody little idiot. Always in a dream, that boy. He's a flipping weirdo, if you ask me.'

I could feel my father tense at all the cursing pouring out of the driver. He squeezed my hand, but I ignored him. We were being
5 driven by a madwoman who had just nearly killed a boy and Father didn't seem bothered by *that* at all!

She looked round at us as if we were supposed to share her outrage, sighed loudly when she got no response and put her foot down. We went through a gateway and over something metal which
10 made the car rattle like crazy and sounded as if we had burst all the tyres.

'Cattle grid,' she explained, trying to catch our eyes in her mirror, and then I screamed again. A cluster of shapes ahead in the road, eyes flashing in the headlights.
15 'Bloody cattle!' she muttered. 'Always in the bloody road. You'd think they own the place.' She wound down her window and started shouting at them. 'Get on, you lummocks!'

They didn't move, apart from a bit of shuffling, their breath hanging in looping white clouds.
20 'Aww, you buggers!' She got out of the car and went to chase them away. They tossed their heads and stood their ground until she got right up to them and then they spun round and galloped off up the road and disappeared.

It made me forget about feeling sick, which was lucky as Bea went
25 back to driving like a maniac the moment the cattle were gone, but I was glad when she swung the car off the road and switched off the engine.

---

1 **bloody** *(inf)* damn – 2 **flipping** *(inf)* damn – 3 **to tense** to become uneasy – 3 **to curse** to complain angrily about sth using rude language – 8 **outrage** anger – 10 **to burst** to break, to explode – 13 **cluster of** group of – 17 **lummocks** *(sl) here:* clumsy, stupid cattle – 18 **to shuffle** to move your feet without really walking – 20 **bugger** *(vulg sl)* stupid or annoying person or thing – 25 **maniac** a mad person

'Yer tis,' she said as she climbed out. 'Your holiday home. Mind the mud. There's a lot of it about.'

She laughed, but not in a kind way.

It was hard to see where the mud was, but I found it almost
5 immediately. One shoe disappeared with a wet squelch and I had to balance on one leg while I groped about to find it. Nice.

'What's you getting up to here, then, Professor?' She said it as if she did not believe Father was a professor at all. 'You trying to get some of our rain over to your neck of the woods?'

10 She laughed again and didn't seem to be interested in an answer. I dug my nails into my hand and hoped I'd never, ever have to see her again.

Then her tone changed. 'Ah. Here's Mrs Wonnacott.' She opened her door and leaned out. 'Got 'em, Mrs W. All yours!'

15 Mrs Wonnacott was quite young and very thin, almost scarily thin. In the torchlight, her face looked more like a skull. She was wearing a knitted hat, so I could not see her hair. I felt a stab of pain. She reminded me of Mama.

We followed her down a path and into a low, dark house that
20 smelled of cooking and something else I could not identify.

There was stuff everywhere. Cardboard boxes, heaps of magazines, books, leaflets.

There was nowhere to put our suitcases, so we just stood inside the door and waited for her to do something.

25 'Welcome to Hope Cottage. I'm afraid it's rather a mess!'

She sounded as if she were only just realising that everything was all over the place and did not care that much.

I stared at her. She kept her hat on, even though it was quite warm in her house. I could see a fire burning in the next room. Her
30 cheekbones stuck out of her face so that you could see their whiteness behind her pale skin and she had no eyebrows. She

---

1 **Yer tis** *(inf, local dialect)* Here it is – 1 **to mind sth** to be careful of sth – 2 **mud** *Matsch* – 6 **to grope** to search – 9 **neck of the woods** *(idm, inf)* place where sb comes from – 16 **skull** *Totenkopf* – 17 **stab** a sudden, sharp feeling – 31 **pale** almost white

looked terrible and I realised that I had been right. She was just like my mama. In the worst possible way.

I turned to Father and stared at him in disbelief. He seemed not to have noticed that this woman was as sick as Mama had been.

5 The woman caught my eye and without thinking, a question came out of my mouth.

'Are you going to die?'

Father let out a gasp. 'Zaynab!'

She ignored him and smiled broadly at me.

10 'I sincerely hope not! I've been told that I'm nearly cured.'

My mother had said the very same thing.

I closed my eyes and then I vomited.

---

9 **broadly** widely – 10 **sincerely** really, truly – 10 **cured** well again – 12 **to vomit** to throw up *(sich erbrechen)*

ZAYNAB

How had my father wiped Mama from his memory as if she'd never existed? He didn't talk about her. I never saw him cry. He went back to work just days after she had gone. He gave away her clothes and most of her books the same week she died.

5 It suddenly dawned on me that we had only ever really spoken to each other when she was there. She was like a bridge between us. Now that bridge was gone. Instead, I had stuff in my head all the time, like an endless conversation being shouted into nothingness.

Mostly, I just wanted to shout at him that it was rubbish, all 10 rubbish. These words came crashing into my head and I could not let them out. I was not sure I even wanted to actually say them. I was just forced to carry them around, like flies in a jar, buzzing and making me feel nauseous.

Mrs Wonnacott told me not to worry about a bit of sick as her 15 cat, Toffee, threw up mice and fur regularly. She took me up to my room, which was in the roof of the cottage with a tiny window. The walls were painted yellow and the bed – a mattress on the floor – was covered in a brightly coloured bedspread with tiny mirrors sewn onto it.

20 'I got that in Kerala,' she said. 'Before I stopped flying.'

'Because of being ill?' I asked.

'No. Because of the planet. Flying is a terrible thing for the planet, so I've stopped travelling.'

She went on, looking awkward, 'But of course, you of all people 25 know all of this, and you and your father could only really get here by plane. Anyway, I expect you are exhausted. The bathroom is on the floor below if you need it, and then you can come and have a bit of supper, if you feel well enough.'

---

5 **to dawn on sb** to become clear – 12 **jar** glass – 13 **nauseous** ['nɔːsiəs] to feel as if you want to vomit – 24 **awkward** ['ɔːkwəd] uneasy, uncomfortable – 26 **exhausted** [ɪg'zɔːstɪd] very tired

She turned to go.

'Where's your husband?' I don't know why I asked that. It just came out ... again.

'My husband? Oh, he's long gone. Collateral damage, you might
5 call it.' She hesitated and I thought she might tell me about him and why and where he had gone, but she just looked at the floor for a moment, flicking the fringe of the rug with her toe.

'Is he dead?' I asked.

'No! No.' She shrugged. 'He's fine. I think.'

10 'My mama is dead,' I replied.

She gave me an intense look before continuing, 'I am so sorry to hear that. I'm guessing from your expression when you saw me that cancer took her from you?'

I nodded.

15 'You must miss her terribly.' She self-consciously pulled at her hat. 'It's almost as tough for the survivors as the sufferers, I know. Maybe even worse. Anyway, come on down when you are ready. I hope you'll like it here. It must be so different from your home.'

She smiled at me and I nearly found myself smiling back.

20 'Call me Deborah, by the way,' she said. 'I haven't felt like Mrs Wonnacott for quite a while.'

When she had gone, I threw myself down on the bed and stared at the roof. A huge cobweb hung down with a dried-up spider in it. I hoped it would not fall on me in the night.

25 From the bathroom I could smell supper and it smelled good. I brushed my teeth to get rid of the sour taste of vomit and sorted out my hijab which had got messed up when we nearly hit the ghost boy. I didn't feel comfortable going without a head-covering in front of this strange woman and I realised that she felt the same, though
30 for completely different reasons.

I left the room and went down the creaky wooden stairs, following the cooking smell. My father was sitting at the kitchen table, drinking

---

5 **to hesitate** to hold back, to be uncertain – 7 **fringe** *Fransen* – 7 **rug** carpet, mat –
16 **tough** hard, difficult

water and talking excitedly about his project and the University, while Deborah tried to clear enough space for plates. She moved a pile of books and papers onto the floor. A large ginger cat appeared and climbed onto the tower of books, which immediately toppled
5   over. The cat looked at me as if to say, 'I meant for that to happen,' and went to sit on one of the books. Deborah shooed it away and rebuilt the pile, leaning it against the wall.

'Toffee does like to cause havoc! Sorry about the mess. There's so much going on … with the campaign.'
10   'What campaign?' I asked.

'Friends of the Earth? You might have heard of us? We campaign on environmental issues. Everything from stopping the extra runway at Heathrow to global cuts in emissions. I am heavily involved in our local group and, to be honest, you being involved in climate
15   science, Professor, made having you here a bit of a no-brainer. In fact, it's a privilege.'

I thought about how Mama had campaigned first to save trees and then for women and girls stuck in the emergency camps, frightened and hungry, whilst Father dreamed up 'eco' projects to
20   let politicians and companies think they were being green.

'I was hoping to set up an Extinction Rebellion branch here, too. If you were to come and speak, that might help kickstart it. We need a bit more genuine activism to get the climate emergency message across. We've been too polite for too long.'
25   'Father isn't an activist. He's paid by the government to come up with tricks to make companies stop polluting everything,' I said. 'Not quite as the Prophet, peace be upon Him, instructed. Mama was the one who actually did things. You know. Really *did* things, useful things that really helped people.'

---

8 **to cause havoc** ['hævək] to make chaos – 12 **environmental** concerned with the protection of the natural world – 12 **issue** an important subject – 13 **emission** release of sth into the atmosphere – 15 **no-brainer** *(inf)* sth, usu a decision, that is easy or obvious – 21 **Extinction Rebellion** a global movement that fights for action to protect the environment and the climate – 21 **branch** office

Father laughed and I could tell he was embarrassed. 'We do Allah's work in different ways. Some less visible than others.'

'Or even invisible,' I retorted.

'Zaynab! We are guests in a stranger's house,' Father hissed.

5 'It's OK,' Deborah interrupted. 'You've had a lot to contend with. You must be feeling very tired and stressed.'

'You don't know how I am feeling,' I said, under my breath.

'You're right.' She gave me a glass of water and I felt bad that she'd heard me. 'As to how we battle the climate emergency, we must all
10 do what we can. Or that's what I think, anyway.'

'Indeed,' my father said. 'We must all do what we can.'

I sat there, my brain boiling with fury at them both – Father just blanking Mama's work; Deborah making so much of her eco warrior thing with her no flying 'sacrifice' and her 'doing what she can'
15 rubbish and thinking we'd be impressed. What did she know of drought and hunger and the bleached bones of cattle in desert that used to be pasture? Nothing. I wanted to shout all this at her. I could feel all the words organising in my head, ready to come out, but then I looked at her pale face and her huge eyes and Mama was
20 back in front of me. Suddenly, I just wanted to be held and have my hair stroked; my anger evaporated away.

Deborah looked straight at me and sort of nodded as if to say, 'I see your pain.'

Maybe she did.

25 I ate a bit of the food. I think it was meant to be a bariis iskukaris, a dish of rice, lamb and spices, but there was no lamb and although it smelled good, the spices were not strong enough and it tasted to me like a bland mush.

Father ate his with enthusiasm, which might have been real or
30 fake. I couldn't tell. I guess she had tried to please us. It was a shame she had omitted the star ingredient.

---

1 **Allah** name of God in Islam – 3 **to retort** to reply angrily – 5 **to contend** to deal with, to fight – 13 **to blank** to deliberately ignore sth – 14 **sacrifice** ['sækrɪfaɪs] sth you give up – 17 **pasture** grassland, meadow – 28 **bland** unexciting, boring – 28 **mush** *Pampe* – 31 **to omit** to leave out

'I'm vegan,' Deborah said, as if reading my mind.

'No caano geel, then?' I asked.

'Sorry? You've lost me there!' she said.

'Camel milk,' Father explained, flashing me a furious look.

'No!' she laughed. 'No camel milk to be had in Devon, though I think you can get it in London. It'll get to us eventually! In the meantime, I can make you some hot cows' milk with cardamom, if you would like?'

She was trying her best. I felt shamed.

'Shukraan. Thank you. That would be nice. You are very kind.'

'It will all be OK, dearest one,' Father said, soothingly. 'Wait and see. This will be good for you and for me, Allah willing. Shall we perform Maghrib together? It is a little late, but not haram.'

I shook my head. 'No. I prefer to pray alone.'

Deborah was trying hard to look busy making my hot milk, but I knew she could sense the tension.

I asked if I could take my drink to my room but, as I shut the kitchen door behind me, I decided to lurk outside and listen to their conversation. I was sure they would talk about me and I was right.

First my father apologised and Deborah replied that it was OK, she'd been a difficult teenager once and it couldn't be easy for me, losing my mother (who I hero-worshipped, apparently) at such an important stage of my life etc. Then they fell silent.

'You and Zaynab speak incredibly good English,' she said, after a while.

'Yes. My wife, my late wife and I met here, in the UK, in Bristol, where I studied at the University. She came from Ireland, originally. She had the most glorious flame red hair ...'

He tailed off and fell silent and I knew that he, too, had a picture of Mama in his head. Mama with her wild mane of fiery curls and her green, green eyes.

Father coughed before continuing. 'Anyway, Zaynab was born here in the UK and Fran always spoke to Zaynab in English at home.'

---

13 **Maghrib** an Islamic evening prayer – 13 **haram** forbidden by Islamic law – 18 **to lurk** to wait secretly – 22 **to hero-worship** to admire sb a lot

'When did your wife die? If you don't mind me asking ...'

'Nearly eight months ago. It is still raw. I do not know when it will not be. And Zaynab seems so angry.'

Still raw? You behave as if it is long forgotten. And if you know I
5 *am angry, why don't you talk to me?* I felt the words form in my head, like burning hot needles.

'Well, if you or Zaynab ever need anyone to talk to ... no, really.' Father must have been shaking his head, but Deborah continued in her calm, clear voice, 'I'm on the road to recovery, but I know
10 about the anger and what it does to people and their lives and I don't mind talking about it. If it would help. Strangers are sometimes easier to talk to, aren't they?'

There was a long silence.

'I thank you for your kind hospitality. I am very tired and I have
15 an early start.' Father sounded very stiff and formal all of a sudden and I knew he felt he had gone too far, said too much. And he had. It was none of her business. It was mine and his.

I crept up the stairs, trying to avoid making them creak. I checked my phone to get the correct direction before saying the evening
20 prayer. I thought Father might knock on my door to say goodnight, but he didn't and saved me the trouble of pretending to be asleep.

The dead spider swung gently in a draught, a tangle of bunched up, see-through legs. I promised myself that I would find something long enough to reach it and get it gone. In the morning.

---

14 **hospitality** friendly, welcoming behaviour towards guests – 17 **to be none of sb's business** *(idm)* to not need to know about sth – 22 **draught** [drɑːft] breeze, wind

LUCAS

I would never, ever forget the day Zaynab arrived in my school and in my life.

The head, Mrs Baldwin, came into class with her one day, three weeks into my second year at 'big school' (as my mum still insisted
5 on calling it). Year Eight.

She was tall, taller than me anyway, and slim, almost thin, with a narrow face and sharp cheek bones and really big eyes with long black lashes, like a deer or a Jersey cow (and I really didn't mean that rudely. Jersey cows are beautiful). Her head and neck were
10 covered by a yellow scarf which looked super bright against her skin. She had the sort of skin colour that my sister, Lara, tried to fake, except that Lara came out streaked with orange.

Mrs Baldwin had her hands on Zaynab's shoulders as she announced her name and I could tell Zaynab wanted to wriggle
15 free. And I could tell that Mrs Baldwin said her name wrong because Zaynab pulled a face when she said it, rolling her eyes to the ceiling.

'This is Zaynab Egal. Zaynab has moved here all the way from Somalia.'

'Somaliland. Not Somalia. They're not the same.' Zaynab said
20 every word carefully and precisely. She sounded really posh.

Mrs Baldwin went stony-faced, before saying, coldly, 'Somaliland. Indeed.'

'Not that it matters,' Zaynab continued, walking away from Mrs Baldwin to the one free desk, three from mine to the right. 'Because
25 I very much doubt anyone here either knows or cares where Somalia or Somaliland are. But then, I did not care where Devon was, so ...'

She shrugged and then sat down and began to take her things out of her bag. Pens. A calculator. The usual stuff. Nothing exciting or different.

---

3 **head** *abbr of* headteacher – 4 **to insist** to say very clearly and firmly – 8 **deer** *Reh, Hirsch* – 16 **ceiling** *Zimmerdecke* – 20 **precisely** exactly – 20 **posh** of a high social class

'Welcome, Zaynab!' Mrs Chadwick, our class teacher, said enthusiastically. 'I can now tick you off on the register!'

None of us said anything. It was like we were frozen. We were all watching as she took out a tablet attached to a solar power bank
5 and then sat, staring ahead of her, her yellow scarf hiding her ears and cheeks, her jaw set hard so that she looked almost like a statue. We weren't sure how to react. I could not tell if she was shy, angry, anxious or just not interested at all. She certainly wasn't friendly, but then neither were we.

10 Mrs Baldwin looked round at us as if she was seeing us all for the first time and didn't particularly like what she saw.

'Please make Zaynab as welcome as you can,' she said in the same cold tones. 'I am sure you'll have lots of questions for her, but she's here to learn about how we do things and to make the most of her
15 brief stay, so let's show her what Devon has to offer, shall we?'

And with that, she left the room, almost slamming the door behind her.

That was when Rich Wells blurted out, 'You a pirate?' and we all cringed with embarrassment.

20 Zaynab swivelled round to see who had spoken. The look she gave him could have sunk a ship.

'Nah. That's Somalia, innit. You a smuggler or a farmer? Cos everyone on Dartmoor's a smuggler or a farmer, am I right?'

She spoke in a completely different voice, copying Rich's Devon
25 accent.

Rich laughed nervously. 'Sorry. I just saw on the TV once and ...' His voice tailed off.

Man, it was tense. Her face had sunk Rich's ship and her voice had dropped the temperature in the room several degrees. She was
30 definitely cool. Really cool. But also scary ... and maybe more than a bit mean.

After class, I thought about showing her the way to the dining room, but she went off in a different direction and then disappeared

---

8 **anxious** [ˈæŋkʃəs] worried, concerned – 18 **to blurt out** to say sth suddenly and without thinking

through a door into what I thought was a storeroom. Maybe she did not want to eat with us?

I waited around for a bit and then gave up and went to lunch. After about ten minutes, she appeared, got some lunch and went to sit at the back of the dining room on her own. I thought about moving to sit with her, but then everyone would have teased me and said I wanted to get off with her, so I watched her from where I sat, hoping she wouldn't notice.

Which, of course, she did.

She fixed me with a stare like an eagle's whilst she stabbed at a pasta salad as if she wanted to kill it. I had to pretend to be looking at something beyond her, which was stupid because there was only a blank wall and when she turned her head to see if there was something interesting there, she knew for sure I had been staring at her. She laughed, soundlessly. It felt like a sneer.

I went back to my lunch. It tasted like dust. Not that I have ever eaten dust.

I'd never seen anyone like her. Even then, I felt she was special, a superhuman come to Earth to teach us something. Something hard and painful. Maybe that was a stupid thought, but that's how I saw her.

It was history after lunch.

Before the lesson started, Mr Reeves got the big globe off the windowsill and asked Zaynab to come and show everyone where Somaliland was. She shrugged and said it was pointless. It wouldn't even be on the map. Mr Reeves looked a bit bewildered and then he asked her if she'd tell us a bit about her home when she felt ready to do so.

'I can tell you now,' she said, getting up and going to the front of the class. She waited until everyone was quiet before speaking. She was so brave. There's no way I would have stood up in front of a load of total strangers.

---

15 **sneer** mocking smile or remark – 16 **dust** *Staub* – 26 **bewildered** confused, surprised

'I am from a country which you British used to rule. Now you do not even say we exist, so we aren't on your map.'

'Perhaps you could tell us a bit about home and your school, Zaynab?' Mr Reeves asked gently.

She said nothing, but started counting how many of us there were in the class. Twenty-eight.

'Fourteen of you, eleven girls and three boys – you can go and stand in the corner and look at the wall. You aren't at school. You're too poor and you live in a camp. You used to live on farms or move from place to place with your animals, but then the droughts came every year and all your crops and animals died and when the rains came, they swept all the soil away. So you have nothing.'

No one moved a muscle. She shrugged her shoulders and started back towards her desk.

I stood up and went into the corner.

'Please can I not turn my back?' I asked. 'I want to hear everything.'

Two girls joined me, the twins Poppy and Daisy.

'Please go on, Zaynab,' Mr Reeves said. 'I think everyone is just a bit stunned. Come on, let's do this properly. Let's have two more boys and nine more girls standing in the corner. Zaynab is trying to teach us about the life chances for children in her country. I, for one, am really saddened to think that Lucas, Daisy, Poppy and the others would miss out on school, miss out on a future, aren't you?'

'I'd choose not to go to school!' someone said. 'That's why I'm standing up.'

'Don't you get it?' Zaynab said. 'You don't have any choices when you are poor.'

'So how come you're here? Have you got lots of money, or something?' Rich Wells asked.

Zaynab shook her head.

'Lucky, then?' someone else added.

She shook her head again.

---

1 **to rule** to control – 11 **crop** plant such as wheat and potatoes that is grown in large quantities by farmers – 19 **to be stunned** to be shocked and surprised

'I do not think I am lucky to be here and not at home, where I belong, but you? You're all lucky and you don't even know it.'

'We had some floods here, too,' Poppy said. 'We know about climate change. It happens here, as well.'

5 Zaynab laughed, but it was not a very nice laugh. Then she stared at us for a while before going back to her seat.

Mr Reeves thanked her: 'Thank you for sharing that, Zaynab. I think we have a lot to learn from you. I hope you will talk to us again very soon.'

10 She shrugged and started doodling in her notebook.

I felt sick with fear and a sort of excitement. She was one angry person and she was going to mess up our lives for sure. Maybe in a good way.

12 **to mess up** *here:* to muddle up, to change

LUCAS

It was sausage and mash for tea. The sausages were fatty and jets of oil burst out through my fork holes making me feel sick. Mum gave me a look as if to say, 'Don't you dare spit out your food!' as I swallowed chunks down without chewing, washed down with a
5   gulp of water.

'I think I'd like to be a vegetarian,' I said, cautiously, waiting for the explosion.

'Hah!' snorted Dad. 'Why? Because you don't like sausages? Fussy. That's what you are.'

10   'It's not just that. It's that meat is bad for the planet.'

'Bad for the planet? You've had your head filled with nonsense, boy.'

'Perhaps we should eat less meat. Or local meat?' Mum said, trying to keep the peace.

15   Dad reached over and stabbed my second sausage.

'Here. I'll help you out. Vegetarian indeed. There are people who'd bite your hand off for a bit of meat. I heard about that foreign kid at school. Scrawny creature, half-starved, Stu said. One of them refugees they've sent us. Suppose her dad'll be taking a job off of
20   one of us soon enough. Country's full already without them lot coming here. Thought we'd stopped all that with Brexit.'

I looked down at my plate with its pool of grey fat already drying on the last of my mash, a nasty sludgy mess. I hated Dad when he was like this. Lashing out at people he did not even know.

25   'She's in my class. She's from Somaliland.'

'Never heard of it,' Dad said, scraping his plate so that it made a screeching noise.

---

1 **mash** mashed potato – 1 **jet** thin stream – 5 **gulp** a large amount of sth –
6 **cautiously** carefully – 8 **fussy** to be difficult to please – 18 **half-starved** nearly dying
from lack of food – 19 **refugee** sb who has been forced to leave their home or
country – 21 **Brexit** act of the UK leaving the European Union – 24 **to lash out** to speak
about sb very angrily or critically

'It's not on the maps.'

'Not on the maps? What are you talking about? You've fallen for some rare old nonsense, by the sound of it.' Dad wiped up the last of his gravy with his finger and licked it noisily.

Lara pushed her plate away and got up to leave the table. I hoped she might say something, but she just sighed as she left the room and muttered, 'God, how I love happy families.'

It was my turn to clear the table and I scraped the rest of my meal into the food waste bin – another thing Dad hated, complaining that he hadn't got time for all the sorting and it was stupid having all these bins when all the council did was tip it all into the same hole in the ground, anyway.

Dad stayed stubbornly at the table, watching while I piled everything up and carried it to the sink.

Suddenly his mood seemed to change.

'You can live off of vegetables if you want. Cheaper. Grow them yourself. Plenty of room.'

He waved a hand at the garden, if you could call it a garden. A patch of concrete with a clothes line and some scrubby grass round the edge and a giant buddleia bush covered in dead, brown flowers.

'You can't grow anything now!' Mum interrupted. 'Winter's coming!'

'Rubbish! He can grow all sorts. We grew chard and spinach and leeks every winter when I was a kid. If he wants to be vegetarian, he knows what to do.'

He folded his paper and headed for the sofa and the TV. The kitchen table was now my desk and I had history and maths homework.

When I'd finished, I thought again about what Zaynab had said about her country. I needed to check it out for myself, but Mum's old laptop was only good for Word documents and spreadsheets. It wouldn't even connect to the Internet. My phone was just one of

---

10 **sorting** *here:* separating rubbish – 19 **concrete** cement – 20 **buddleia bush** *Sommerflieder* – 23 **chard** *Mangold* – 24 **leek** *Lauch* – 31 **spreadsheet** a computer program with tables such as Excel

Mum's cast-offs with next to no data and rubbish with our dodgy Wi-Fi. I'd have to ask Lara. I knocked on her door and went in to ask.

'Oh for goodness' sake, get a better phone, why don't you?' Lara
5 barely looked up from her screen as her thumbs flew across it. She never had much energy for anything until it came to messaging her mates. Then she was hyper.

I didn't bother to ask her how she thought I'd get a new smartphone with no money. 'Please! I'll be really quick!'

10 'Don't use up my data,' she said, crossly, as she threw the phone at me. 'Two minutes. Go!'

I googled Somaliland.

It had declared itself to be an independent State but it looked like only Sheffield and Cardiff had said it should be recognised. How
15 weird! Why those cities? Ahh! Because they had big Somalilander communities and had done for ages. Seemed the Government did not recognise the country, though, and the Foreign Office said you shouldn't go there unless you had to, so it must be dangerous. But then another report said there were no figures on crime or terrorism
20 because the country didn't exist and then yet another site said it was really peaceful and democratic and nothing like Somalia.

'Phone!' bellowed Lara, holding out her hand. 'Time's up.'

I gave it back to her, reluctantly. I had been about to read an article on the droughts. Still, at least I had something sensible to
25 ask Zaynab if I ever managed to speak to her. Something that would show her I was really interested and not just nosy.

The last image I'd seen was of a sheep skull bleached white, half buried in dried, cracked soil and I thought of the sheep up on the moors, their legs and feet black from the mud. They had problems,
30 for sure, but dying from lack of water wasn't one of them.

---

1 **cast-off** a thing that is no longer wanted – 1 **dodgy** (*inf*) unreliable, of low quality – 10 **crossly** angrily, annoyed – 23 **reluctantly** unwillingly, hesitantly – 26 **nosy** too interested in other people's business

ZAYNAB

Week two and the ride into school was turning out to be the worst
part of each day. By the time it got to me, the bus was three-quarters
full. There were some stupid boys, couple of years older, who had
teased me about my hijab, offered me some kind of bacon flavoured
5   crisps and called me a jihadi until I told them I'd report them. My
teacher back home had told me to expect this kind of thing from
ignorant people. Anyway, these boys weren't a problem anymore.
Unlike the gang of toxic girls.

Every morning the same. Fifteen-year-olds, covered in make-up
10   with their uniform in a mess, showing no respect. Shameless, stupid,
they were giving girls a bad name. Picking on the younger kids?
Pathetic. Pathetic and boring. Even the driver told them to stop
sometimes, but they just ignored him.

'Oh, here she is! Zaynab, come from Wakanda to teach us all a
15   lesson!'

'Where's your spear? Where's your camel?'

'When you going home, immigrant?'

This last comment was from their leader, a blonde girl with a skirt
so short it could not possibly be within the rules. Ella Chambers.

20   I put my headphones on and stared out of the window. The rain
just kept coming. The road was being worn away on either side by
water pouring off the moors. I wished they could see what a real
flash flood looked like, after months of drought. A year's worth of
rain falling in just two days, smashing onto the burnt crust of earth,
25   growing into a giant river, uprooting trees, carrying off everything
in its path, including houses, animals, people.

I could almost wish it on them.

---

7 **ignorant** uninformed, without understanding – 11 **to pick on sb** to criticise sb,
to be nasty to sb – 14 **Wakanda** a fictional country appearing in the Marvel Comics –
17 **immigrant** sb who has come from one country to live in another country –
25 **to uproot** to be pulled out of the ground

Lucas got on at the next stop. Ghost boy. My secret name for him from that first night when the taxi nearly ran him over. He gave me an intense look as he passed me and sat in the seat behind. Maybe today he would actually speak to me. I was the visitor, the guest in
5 his country. He had to make the first move.

Ella was suddenly alongside me. She yanked at my hijab and shouted, 'Watchoo think you look like, terrorist?'

I ignored her.

'Hey! I'm talking to you, terrorist!' she jeered as she knocked off
10 my headphones.

'Leave her alone.' It was Ghost Boy.

'Aww! You standing up for your girlfriend? Oh, wait. You don't have a girlfriend and you never will, Lucarse Loser.'

'You are a very ignorant and stupid girl. How long have you been
15 going to school? Ten years? Still you know nothing!' I said, putting as much contempt into my voice as I could.

The bus driver shouted at us over his shoulder.

'That's enough! Stop making trouble and get back in your own seat.'
20 Ella ignored him.

'You should go back home where you belong, darkie.'

'If you insult me or touch me again,' I said, feeling hatred in my heart and in my throat, 'I will be forced to strike you.'

The bus went totally quiet.
25 The bus driver stopped the bus.

'That's it. Off the bus. Now.'

I got my stuff together and started for the door. Ghost Boy followed me.

'I'm getting off, too,' he said, quietly. 'She was bang out of order.'
30 'Not you. You!' The bus driver pointed at Ella. 'You and your little crew. Off you hop. You're a nasty lot. Need to learn some manners. Go on! I'm not having your sort on my bus.'

---

6 **to yank** (*inf*) to pull sth forcefully – 16 **contempt** a strong feeling of dislike –
21 **darkie** (*off*) a very offensive word for a black person – 23 **to strike** to hit –
31 **nasty** very unpleasant – 31 **lot** (*inf*) group

The other two girls wailed, 'But it's raining!'

'So it is. Go on, off you get, the lot of you. Shouldn't take you more than a couple of minutes from here. You're not welcome on this bus until you can behave.'

'But she threatened me! That's practically assault!' Ella squealed.

'A few words from a younger kid isn't assault. And you had them coming, dearie. Mind the puddles.'

He pulled away from the three girls as they stood in a huddle under an umbrella.

Then he called out to me over his shoulder: 'I don't approve of violence, young lady, even if it's only a threat. Do that again and you'll be walking, too. Understood?'

I nodded.

We sat back down in our seats as if nothing had happened.

I turned to him and whispered, 'Jazakallah, Ghost Boy.'

'Ghost Boy? Why do you call me that? And what's jazakallah?' he asked.

'You're the boy we nearly killed on the road when you popped up like a ghost. Actually, I saved your life by screaming. That taxi woman would have knocked you down. So, Ghost Boy! And "jazakallah" is what we say when we're thanking someone. It means "may God reward you with goodness."'

He blushed a deep red.

'Oh. Well, thank you. I owe you. My real name is Lucas, by the way. Can I sit next to you?'

'Sure. I'd say we were even now, wouldn't you?'

'That was very good, what you did in class,' he said, 'to explain about people not going to school.'

'It's how Mama used to explain things to the CrisisAid charity workers from Europe. She always said it was better to show people, not just tell them. Make it real.'

He nodded. 'We didn't go to school for ages because of Corona-virus. It was horrible. Like being in prison. We all nearly went mad.'

---

5 **assault** attack – 7 **puddle** *Pfütze* – 24 **to owe** to be in debt – 26 **to be even** not in debt

'Yeah, that must have been tough for you people, because no one else had any problems, did they?'

As soon as the sarcastic words were out of my mouth, I felt bad. This boy could not know what life was like for people thousands of miles away.

'It's not a competition to see who has the worst time, though, is it?' I said, trying to sound friendly.

Lucas looked anxious. 'Sorry. I guess it just shows that I have no idea ...' He tailed off.

'Not your fault,' I said. 'How could you know? Come on. We're here.'

The other kids stood aside so that we could get off first. The driver winked at us.

'Let's hope they've learned their lesson, eh?' he said. 'See you later and behave yourselves!'

LUCAS

I couldn't really concentrate in morning lessons. Zaynab disappeared into the storeroom again, but this time I waited for her outside the dining room and we sat together. I picked at my lasagne, trying not to eat any of the meat while she picked at hers.

5 'What do you do in the storeroom?' I asked, tentatively.

'Pray. Next question?'

She did not seem annoyed. Just a bit amused.

'Oh. Well, can I ask about why you're here?'

'Sure. No space in the schools in Exeter. So my father says.' She
10 grimaced. 'But you didn't mean that. Sorry. I am here because wherever my father's work takes him is where I have to go.'

'What's his work?' I asked, watching a scowl appear on her face and then vanish, to be replaced by a blank expression.

'He works with bad companies who want people to think they
15 are good. He thinks up things for them to do, eco-projects and stuff.' She pushed her plate away and drank her water. 'The companies who got the planet into the mess it's in now. Oh, and he teaches at the University of Borama.'

'Oh. So is he teaching at the University in Exeter?"

20 'A bit. And he's working with some company or other on something. It's boring.'

'And your mother? Is she ...?'

'Dead,' Zaynab said, baldly.

'I'm so sorry.' I didn't know what else to say. Zaynab seemed to
25 be trying really hard to stay calm.

After a long silence, I tried to change the subject.

'Do you try to do anything about climate change? You sounded quite annoyed about what your dad does, like it's fake or something.'

---

5 **tentatively** uncertainly, hesitantly – 12 **scowl** angry or hostile expression – 18 **Borama** city in Somaliland

She glared at me. 'It *is* fake. And you should call it a climate emergency, now.' She paused before continuing. 'Mama actually *did* stuff. She took me on protests. She took me to the camps which CrisisAid run. She really helped people and she wasn't frightened of anything or anyone.'

She looked as if she might cry. I couldn't imagine what it would be like without my mum. Just me and Lara and Dad. Terrible!

'I want to really do something, too, so I'm going vegetarian,' I said, before I could stop myself. 'Because mass-produced meat's bad for the planet and the other stuff is too expensive.'

Pathetic! What was I thinking?

'Is that your protest? When I'm guessing you don't like meat, in any case?' she said, looking very pointedly at my plate.

I could feel myself blush as I admitted it.

'It's easy to do good things when they are also what you want to do anyway,' she said.

I wanted to say something that would make her realise that I was serious. Then I remembered.

'You know Greta Thunberg? Some people tried to do a school climate strike here, but Mrs Baldwin, the head, well, she wouldn't let them. She said school was more important than a climate protest.'

Zaynab didn't seem to have heard. She looked as if she was miles away in her head.

The bell went and I got up to clear our plates.

'You say she wouldn't let them?' she asked, suddenly. 'I think it's time to try again. Don't you?'

---

1 **to glare** to look at sb angrily – 14 **to admit sth** to say that sth is true

ZAYNAB

Lucas and I sat together on the bus home so that we could start planning the school strike. Lucas started sketching out a poster showing the planet half on fire and half under water. It was brilliant.

'You're really good at art,' I said, watching as he worked. 'Wish I
5 could do that.'

'And I wish I could stand up in front of people and speak,' he said, shyly, before adding, 'Will your dad be mad when you miss school? Mine will go mental, if he finds out.'

'I won't be telling mine,' I said. 'He doesn't need to know. He
10 wouldn't be interested, anyway.'

Whereas Mama would have wanted to come along, I thought, sadly.

I could hear sniggering from further back in the bus and the occasional shriek of laughter from Ella and her gang.

15 Someone tapped me on my shoulder. *Here we go again* I thought, but I was wrong.

'Hi. Zaynab? Aoife Coleman. That's A.O.I.F.E. Eefa. Just wanted to say, good on you for standing up to Ella. She definitely had it coming. If she ever reports you, I'll back you up. I'm Year Ten. Swap
20 numbers? You can message me if you need me.'

Aoife smiled warmly. I stared at her. She was extraordinary. Her red hair was cropped closely to her head and gelled into a spike at the front and she had a hole in the side of her nose where she must have had a stud. Her black coat was covered with protest badges
25 and patches.

Why hadn't I noticed her before?

She seemed to guess what I was thinking.

'I sit at the back. Of course, d'oh! Like all rebels ... So! What you got there?'

---

8 **to go mental** (*sl*) to go crazy – 13 **sniggering** disrespectful laughing – 24 **stud** type of earring

Lucas showed her the poster.

'Meeting for a school climate strike. Love it. Count me in. I'll bring some others. A couple of kids tried to do this last year. They should have stuck at it and not listened to old Baldy. Fair play to you!'

5 She went back to the rear of the bus and sat down with a bunch of much older kids who looked almost grown up.

I felt myself beaming at Lucas, but he didn't look that pleased.

'That's not good. Aoife Coleman! She's always in trouble. I mean *always*. She's been suspended loads of times.'

10 I was intrigued by her. 'What for?'

'Bunking off. Smoking. Swearing at teachers ... Honestly, Zaynab, she's bad news. Everyone knows. I even knew before I came to this school. She's famous.'

'Yeah, well people can change. And if she wants to join us, why
15 should we stop her? We need people like her. People who don't take any rubbish. And you mean *infamous*, by the way.'

'She'll bring Jack Kerrow and he's bad news, too. You must have seen him around. He's unmissable.'

I hadn't, but I would definitely look out for him now. As to them
20 being bad news, I didn't really care. We had a fight on our hands. We needed fighters.

'You're pretty judgey for a ghost, you know. By the way, your name means "bright" or "shining". I looked it up. Ghost Boy, glowing in the dark,' I joked, trying to bounce him out of his negativity.

25 'And Zaynab? What does that mean?'

The words stuck in my throat for a moment.

'Father's precious jewel. Or fragrant flower. Take your pick.'

I turned away and stared out of the window.

Lucas said nothing and I was glad.

30 We got to his stop and he stood up to go, then hesitated. He looked so anxious!

---

7 **to beam** to smile widely, to grin – 9 **to suspend sb** to temporarily stop sb from going to school – 10 **to be intrigued by sth** to be interested in sth so that you want to know more – 11 **to bunk off** (*inf*) to leave school without being allowed – 16 **infamous** famous for doing sth considered bad – 27 **precious** ['preʃəs] worth a lot, valuable

'I could come back with you and we could finish the poster and maybe you could get it on Instagram and Snapchat. I only have a crappy phone. And I can walk home. And I won't need any food or anything. But only if it's OK with you.'

5 'Sure.' I smiled at him.

'I could show you the moor, if you like,' he offered, as we set off down the track to Hope Cottage.

'I can see it!' I laughed. 'I see it every day, when it's not too misty or rainy to see anything, like now.'

10 He looked disappointed, then he seemed to set his jaw.

'I meant *really* show you. There are lots of amazing walks round here and you can climb to the tops of the tors and see for miles.'

'Maybe at the weekend?'

He grinned. 'At the weekend. Yes. And we could make a banner
15 for the first school strike?'

I nodded. 'OK, Ghost Boy. You're on.'

Only a couple of weeks in Devon, and I seemed to have got a friend. I hadn't had a true friend for so long. Not since Mama got ill. Now, here I was in a strange place with a strange boy *and* it
20 looked like I would be protesting again, just like I had with Mama.

I felt a sort of glow inside and a sudden surge of energy.

'Race you to the door?' I said, not waiting for an answer, as I ran as fast as I could down the track.

We tumbled in through the front door, out of breath and laughing.
25 And then I saw Deborah, sitting in the kitchen looking drained, with all her meds laid out in front of her and, for an instant, I was back home with Mama.

Deborah tried to look cheerful as she saw me push Lucas towards the study.

30 'Spicy sweet potatoes and squash for supper!' she shouted after us. 'Plenty to go round!'

'Shouldn't we go and say hello?' Lucas asked.

---

12 **tor** a high hill or rock – 25 **drained** worn out, exhausted – 26 **meds** (*inf*) medicine –
30 **squash** a plant that can be eaten (*Speisekürbis*)

I shook my head. 'She's busy. We should leave her alone. Let's do some research on School Strikes for Climate.'

I switched on Father's computer. It was quicker than my tablet and he'd given me his password so that I could use it in an emergency.

I sneaked a peek at his emails. The inbox was full of messages from someone called Anthony at Jurassic Oil and Gas.

'Look at this,' I said. 'While we are planning to protest against polluters and fossil fuel companies, my father is probably doing business with one of them. Let's see what he is up to, shall we?'

Lucas looked uncomfortable.

'I really don't think you should read another person's emails,' he said, nervously.

I shrugged and switched to Google.

'Let's see what Greta is up to, instead.'

Lucas smiled with relief. I could see he was a nice boy. Maybe too nice. We had a battle to fight. He would have to toughen up.

---

6 **to sneak a peek at sth** to secretly have a quick look at sth – 9 **fossil fuel** *fossiler Brennstoff* – 17 **to toughen up** to get braver, stronger

LUCAS

I ran home that evening, feeling really excited and a bit scared. There was something about being with Zaynab that was like the prickle in the air before a thunderstorm combined with the crazy, skippy feeling I sometimes got when I saw the first lambs leaping about in
5   the fields.

'You're late,' said Dad, as he flicked through the channels on TV. 'You've missed your tea. Your mother's upset. She got you something veggie. It wasn't that bad, actually.'

He rubbed his stomach and made lip-smacking sounds before
10 laughing.

'I'm kidding. It's in the microwave. Wouldn't catch me eating that muck.'

I was putting the pack of vegetarian lasagne in the fridge, when Mum came in. 'Aren't you hungry?' she asked, worried. 'I got you
15 that specially.'

'Really sorry, Mum, but I already ate something at a friend's house. I can have this tomorrow. Thank you.'

She looked disappointed.

Dad chortled with laughter. 'Got a friend, now, have we? You took
20 your time! Who is it?'

'Err. Someone new at school. You wouldn't know them.'

As I headed for my room, Dad called after me, 'Not that foreign kid, I hope.'

I didn't reply, but I heard Mum say, 'Why would that matter?'
25 I didn't wait to hear what Dad said.

In my room, I got out all the information that Zaynab had printed off for me. Deborah had given me some leaflets from Friends of the Earth and Extinction Rebellion, or 'XR' as she called them.

---

4 **to leap** to jump – 9 **lip-smacking** *Geschmatze* – 12 **muck** *(inf)* sth regarded as of bad quality or unpleasant

XR were so cool and so determined to force governments into doing something. They blocked traffic and occupied bridges and the protestors really did not care about getting carried out of the way by the police or even arrested. I was pretty sure Mum and Dad
5 would absolutely forbid me to get involved with them.

I couldn't really believe that Mrs Wonnacott – Deborah – would be prepared to do the sorts of things XR did. She seemed so kind and gentle and not a rebel type at all, but she told us about the training she'd been on to handle being put in jail or staying safe if
10 a demo turned violent. She really seemed like she would do anything to get a good result for the planet.

'People are angry and the messages aren't getting through,' she'd explained. 'We don't advocate violence in any circumstance, but things can go wrong if troublemakers turn up and try to provoke a
15 response.'

Deborah could really help us with our campaign. I couldn't understand why Zaynab was being weird with her. She did everything she could to avoid actually looking at or talking to Deborah and didn't seem to be listening at all, even though it was important
20 stuff. In fact, I'd say she was ignoring her. She ate her tea as quickly as she could and tried to make me eat fast, too. In the end, she seemed to get exasperated and left the room while I was still finishing.

'It's difficult for Zaynab to be around me,' Deborah had said. 'I
25 remind her too much of her mum … even down to this campaigning. I don't know if she has told you, but her mum died of cancer. Different kind from me, and I'm expecting to get the all-clear, but nobody likes to be around sick people at the best of times. This is extra hard.'

30 'I think her mum was really important to her,' I said. 'She talks about her a lot.'

---

1 **to be determined** to have a strong wish to do sth – 2 **to occupy** to take over, to control – 9 **jail** prison, place where criminals are kept – 13 **to advocate** to support – 22 **exasperated** annoyed – 27 **the all-clear** *here:* confirmation that she has recovered from cancer

Deborah agreed. 'I know. But it's good that she's got you as a friend. Really good. I don't think she's nearly as tough and independent as she makes out.'

Maybe she wasn't. I didn't really know her, yet. She seemed pretty 5 tough on her dad. She had somehow got into his email account and was going to read his emails, but I think I looked really horrified, so she'd stopped.

'Do you really think we can make a difference?' I'd asked as I joined Zaynab in the study again, trying to change the mood as she 10 scrolled through the Fridays for Future website.

She turned to me, her eyes blazing.

'Of course we can. Father used to tell Mama that she was wasting her time when she camped out to stop trees being cut down, but she saved them. They are still standing because she did something. 15 If we do nothing, or wait for other people to do something, it'll be game over. We have to do whatever it takes.'

She scanned my face as if she was trying to work out whether I was really worth bothering with or not.

'Mama had a motto – no "if onlys". That means never saying "If 20 only I'd done this or not done that." That's how I am going to live my life. What about you?'

I thought for a moment. I thought about all the stuff I hadn't done in case something went wrong. She was watching me closely and could see me hesitating.

25 'It's all right,' she said, calmly. 'You aren't like me. That's good. I'll make you go faster and further but you'll keep me safe. Like stopping me from looking at Father's emails. That was good. I need you for that.'

Now, I lay on my bed and thought about what Zaynab had said. 30 Would I do whatever it took? Was I brave enough? I wondered what Mum and Dad would do if I got arrested, but would the police arrest kids? I felt a bit sick. What was I getting myself into?

11 **to blaze** to glow, to shine

LUCAS

In the end there were only nine of us at the planning meeting for
our Fridays for Future strike. I could tell Zaynab was disappointed,
even though she tried hard to hide it. Aoife and Jack, a tall thin boy
around fifteen, and a girl about the same age. No one from our class
5 until, just as Zaynab was about to start, the doors flew open and the
twins burst in.

'Ready, willing and able to save the planet!' said Poppy, breath-
lessly, pretending to salute Zaynab.

'God help us!' groaned Aoife. 'The gruesome twosome.'

10 'This is so cool, because we've been, like, freaking about climate
change and we are really into activism,' Daisy enthused.

'We made banners and placards and we were on Channel 4 News.
The media loves twins,' boasted Poppy.

'Who even cares?' Aoife interrupted, 'and which one of you is
15 which, anyway?'

'I'm Poppy! My hair's, like, blonder than Daisy's. See?'

Aoife snorted. 'Name badges would be easier.'

I could see Zaynab was beginning to get annoyed.

'Why are you here? Any of you? Why?' she asked.

20 'Like I said,' started Poppy, 'we really care about the planet and
we want to stop climate change.'

'Emergency,' I said. 'It's an emergency, now.'

'Dude's right.' Jack stretched his arms behind his head and
managed to speak and yawn at the same time. 'My dad says it's an
25 emergency and our politicians are doing nothing. Just talking and
promising. It's all garbage and we are so done.'

'We only eat organic. And we recycle. I mean like everything. We
buy those huge bottles of shampoo and stuff because it's less plastic.'

---

3 **even though** although *(obgleich)* – 9 **gruesome twosome** *(inf)* the terrible two –
11 **to enthuse** to talk about sth in a way that shows how excited you are – 12 **placard**
poster – 13 **to boast** to speak very proudly *(prahlen)* – 24 **to yawn** *gähnen*

This was from a girl with big, round glasses, who said her name was Sophie-Ann. She was in Year Ten. While she was speaking, another girl from our class slunk into the room. Izzy Anderson. Even more shy than me.

5 'We use shampoo in a bar, like soap, so that's no plastic at all,' Daisy said, smugly.

'Jeez!' Aoife stood up. 'What even is this? Some kinda flipping competition? I only use planet friendly this and organic that, blah, blah, blah. It's all virtue signalling rubbish. You're all consumers.
10 You're consuming rubbish. They're marketing it to you to make you feel good. You don't even need to wash your hair. It's all just garbage like Jack says.'

Sophie-Ann spoke again: 'I tried to organise a school strike last year, but Mrs B stopped us.'

15 'You bottled it, you mean,' Aoife said contemptuously.

Sophie-Ann shrugged. 'Think what you like. It didn't happen. Let's hope we can get it past her this time.'

Zaynab was watching them, saying nothing herself. She had that eagle look on her face.

20 Then she spoke, cutting off Aoife having a go at Sophie-Ann. There was something in Zaynab's voice – a kind of energy – that made everyone else pay attention, even though we were the juniors in the room.

'Why are you here?' she repeated. There was a short silence.

25 'Because I care,' the tall, thin boy spoke. 'I care and I don't want anybody to say that I didn't bother to do anything. That I let it all be destroyed. Because we are killing and poisoning everything and we have got to make it all stop.'

Zaynab nodded in approval.

30 'We need to do something to get people's attention. I mean –' she looked round the room – 'this is pathetic, right? Nine of us. Out of a total of six hundred and fifty.'

---

6 **smugly** self-satisfied, contently – 9 **virtue signalling** attempt to show others you are a good person by expressing opinions you think will be acceptable to them – 15 **to bottle it** *(inf)* to have lost courage at the last moment – 15 **contemptuously** [kən'temptʃuəsli] *opp of* approvingly *(verachtungsvoll)* – 29 **approval** agreement

'Less than two per cent.' This was from the thin boy, whose name was Rudy Harris. 'Dire.'

'I know people who said they were coming,' added Sophie-Ann.

'Talk is cheap. That's what my dad says.' Jack seemed pretty keen
5 on what his dad said.

'It is. It's cheap and meaningless,' Zaynab agreed.

'So what *are* we doing here?' asked Daisy.

'We are joining the Fridays for Future campaign. And we are going to stage a school strike. Next Friday.' Zaynab's eyes flashed with
10 excitement.

'Why don't you tell them why *you* are doing this, Zaynab?' I asked, shyly. 'I'm here because of you and your story, really.'

Zaynab gave me a big smile and then, just as quickly, it became a frown.

15 'It's not about me,' she said, firmly.

'OK, OK,' Aoife interrupted. 'But you're the only one of us who has really seen what climate change can do. My auntie got flooded two winters ago, but it was just smelly carpets and a load of mess. It didn't ruin her life. She didn't starve.'

20 Zaynab took a deep breath and then she told us all about her mother's work. 'It's really hard to explain what it is like to lose everything. I only know a bit about it because I've seen it. Families in a shack made of corrugated iron that gets scorching hot during the day. No water. No power. No loo. No privacy. No safety.'

25 Poppy and Daisy squeaked, 'Euww.'

'Imagine seeing your animals starving to death. Imagine leaving your house, your farm, and taking only the few things you can carry and then imagine walking further than going to the moors and back ten times to try to find food. And all because rich countries have
30 been pumping out greenhouse gases without thinking what it does to us. You look outside and it's all green. You turn on your tap and

---

2 **dire** terrible, awful – 4 **talk is cheap** (*idm*) it is easy to say that one will do sth –
9 **to stage** to organize – 14 **frown** a facial expression that shows sb is annoyed, sad or
thinking hard – 23 **shack** simple hut – 23 **corrugated iron** *Wellblech* – 23 **scorching hot**
extremely hot – 24 **loo** (*inf*) toilet – 30 **greenhouse gases** *Treibhausgase*

you can drink the water that comes out of it. You can go to a proper loo and lock the door. Things you do here might not wreck your lives, but they destroy ours. That's the bit *you* don't get.'

When she had finished, she had a faraway look about her and I
5   guessed she was back home in her head. We didn't know what to say. It was embarrassing. Then she seemed to snap back into our world and into a different kind of mood.

'I think we should occupy the space by the Town Hall. Nobody will see us if we do it outside school. It's too far from a main road.
10 And, anyway, Greta said it's best to be outside a government building.'

Izzy was wide-eyed. 'You mean, we don't go to school?'

'School strike! What do you think that means, brainbox?' Aoife's voice was full of contempt.
15 'Maybe we should get permission?' said Daisy.

'No.' Zaynab was very definite. 'They might refuse. We just do it. This is a rebellion. Are you in or out?'

'I'm worried about getting into trouble,' Izzy said, wringing her hands so that the knuckles showed white.
20 Aoife rolled her eyes. 'Some rebel you'll be!'

'We need the media to take notice,' said Rudy, 'otherwise, it'll be a waste of time.'

'You should film it,' Sophie-Ann said and then, when she caught the look on Zaynab's face, 'I mean, I will film it. Then we can post
25 on Insta and TikTok.'

'Great. Friday, then. Straight off the bus and into position outside the Town Hall. Tell everyone you can.' Zaynab shut her notebook. 'Is there anything else we need to do?'

'I brought an old sheet,' Aoife said. 'Thought we could make a
30 banner ... or at least decide what goes on it?'

Zaynab nodded approvingly.

'And I've found videos of chants we can do,' added Sophie-Ann. 'We need to make a noise.'

---

2 **to wreck** to destroy, to ruin – 14 **contempt** disrespect, feeling that sb or sth is worthless – 32 **chant** a slogan or phrase that is repeated over and over again

'I'll bring my bodhrán,' Aoife responded, gleefully. I'm sure she
knew we had absolutely no idea what a 'borran' was and was longing
for us to ask, but, by then, the twins were chattering excitedly about
what they were going to wear and I could see that Zaynab was trying
5 to shut out their noise and focus on Greta Thunberg's Instagram.

I wondered what I could bring to make our protest more eye-
catching. I didn't think Mum would be very happy if I nicked one
of our bed sheets, but maybe I could borrow a pan to bash. It would
be hard to smuggle it out without anyone asking questions. Then I
10 remembered Dad's old survival kit from when he and his mates
used to play at soldiers on the moors and that gave me an idea. I
muttered 'yes!' under my breath.

'You got a surprise up your sleeve?' Rudy asked.

'Not really. My dad's got some face paint we could use, that's all.'
15 'Face paint?' scoffed Aoife. 'We're not having flipping butterflies
and tigers on our faces. It's not a flipping fete!'

'He knows that,' Rudy said, winking at me. 'Don't you, mate?'

I liked Rudy. He was cool and friendly and kind. Someone you
could trust.
20 When they'd all gone, I asked Zaynab if she thought it was weird
that everyone had let her be in charge, without any kind of challenge
at all, when she was one of the youngest in the room.

She looked at me as if it had never occurred to her that it should
be any other way.
25 I guess that was what made her a leader.

1 **bodhrán** ['baʊrɒn] a drum popular in Irish and Scottish folk music – 1 **gleefully**
happily – 8 **pan** *Pfanne*

ZAYNAB

On Friday morning, when we got off the bus and I walked in the opposite direction from school and towards the Town Hall, I felt power and anger run through me like an electrical storm over the desert.

5   How many would follow us? How many had the courage? We should have done posters and told more people, maybe, but if anyone else had been really interested, they would have come to the meeting.

   Lucas had brought a tin of greasy black, brown and green camo
10 paint he had stolen-stroke-borrowed from his father. We marked ourselves like warriors.

   A couple of people stopped to watch as Aoife and Jack unfolded the banner which they had made from an old sheet, just as they had promised. It said, *Fridays for Future. School Strike for the Climate*
15 and had the Extinction Rebellion symbol. They had done well. It was bold and strong and said exactly what Greta said it should. No one could miss it.

   Sophie-Ann crossed the street to get a good photo. Rudy Harris ran to catch up with us. Behind him was a little kid. How had she
20 got here?

   'Sorry. My sister, Kitty. Couldn't stop her.'

   How had the driver not seen her get on the bus? A six-year-old kid! Damn. It was not a day for babies and I was not a babysitter.

   She stared at me without blinking, then she tore off her jacket.
25 She was wearing a yellow T-shirt that she had written on: *Don't steel my lif*, it said, in red glitter pen. Nice.

   'You'd better not cry or want snacks or to go peepee all the time,' I said. 'I'm not going to be your mama.'

   She narrowed her eyes and set her jaw.

5 **courage** bravery, ability to control your fear in a difficult situation – 9 **camo** *abbr of* camouflage (*Tarnung*)

'I want to fight. For Greta. For me.' She pulled off her beanie. Her blonde hair was in two straight plaits. She stared at me again. Blue eyes as deep as the skies back home.

OK. Cool kid.

5 I grabbed the camo paint from Lucas and stuck two fingers in the black, swiping two stripes across Kitty's pink cheeks. I gave her my fiercest stare. She did not even twitch.

'I see you, my sister,' I said and held out my hand for a high five.

She could hit hard. She had more guts than any of them, that was 10 clear.

Izzy? No. She was walking fast towards school. She looked back at us for a moment. I could tell she was ashamed. 'Chicken!' I shouted. She just walked faster and disappeared round the corner.

'Go, then! We don't need you!' I shouted.

15 Lucas turned away in embarrassment. He needed to toughen up for sure. There was no way the war would be won if we just played nice all the time.

We tied the banner to a stone tub that stood below the noticeboard outside the Town Hall's main door. I read the bits of paper pinned 20 up behind the glass. Salsa classes. Learn Spanish. Yoga. Art lessons. Nothing about anything that mattered. The house was on fire and people were dancing and drawing as if they had no idea what was coming.

The twins appeared. I had forgotten about them. They'd made a 25 flag copying Lucas's planet design, which he'd showed them at the meeting. It was pretty cool.

The shops were beginning to open. People stared at us but said nothing, just carried on as if it were normal for there to be kids covered in camouflage paint and slogans, out on the street and not 30 in school.

I could feel the anger and excitement rising in my throat. I wanted to shout and wake these people up.

---

2 **plait** *Zopf* − 7 **to twitch** to make a sudden small movement (*zucken*) − 9 **guts** *(pl, inf)* will and courage to do sth which is difficult or unpleasant − 21 **to matter** to be important or relevant

Maybe Aoife could see I needed noise. She pulled out a big flat disc covered in animal hide and a stick like a wooden dog bone from her rucksack. I immediately felt homesick. I wished I had my yoome drum, a beautiful thing with tooled leather and taut skin, decorated with orange tassels. Aoife's looked plain. Almost ugly.

But, wow! She could play that thing. The bone beater twisted in her hands as she hit the drum with alternate ends and it was loud. It made my heart beat faster.

Kitty started whooping and jumping around. She looked so wild, so free. Not like a white English doll with her blonde plaits, but like a spirit or a demon.

Soon we all became like Kitty. We caught her joy like a disease. Even my anger became joyful.

We were there. We were alive. We were protesting.

We danced until we were warm, stamping our feet and singing.
'People gonna rise like the water!
Gonna shut this system down!
Hear the voice of your great-granddaughter
Saying "Climate justice NOW!"'

It felt good. So good.

A couple of people tooted their horns as they drove by. Yeah. Pro the planet but driving diesels. Still, the toots felt good, too.

Every now and then I shouted, 'Give us back our future!' My voice bounced off the walls of the narrow street and made shoppers turn their heads to stare.

We kept singing and dancing. If I stopped for a moment, the others stopped, too. Without me, they would do nothing, say nothing. I danced more wildly, Kitty following me like a shadow as I whirled and circled the others. I remembered dancing with Mama and women and girls at one of the camps. I could almost hear her laughter, her joy. I could see the faces of the children – Idil, Asha, Faduma. I wished I was with them now.

And then the magic was broken by an old man shouting.

---

4 **taut** tightly stretched – 5 **tassel** pieces of wool or other materials tied together at one end and attached as decorations (*Quaste*)

LUCAS

'What do you think you're doing? Stop that racket! Take that banner down!'

The man's voice was aggressive and he started to tug at the banner as if he wanted to tear it up, then he let go of it in disgust and
5 frustration and turned to Zaynab. He stood too close to her. Dangerously close. For him. Not her.

I put my hand on her arm to try to stop her saying or doing anything but before she even opened her mouth, Aoife had pushed her aside and confronted the man.

10 'What are we doing? Your job!' she said. 'Now, go away, old man. Your house is on fire. Go piss on it.'

'I'll call the police, is what I'll do. Making this unholy racket! Leaping about like savages! You're all playing truant, the lot of you.'

He looked as if he might explode with fury.

15 Zaynab stepped back in front of Aoife and looked the angry man straight in the eye.

'We are fighting for your future, too,' Zaynab said. 'Why don't you care what happens to the planet?'

The man started spluttering about 'stuff and nonsense' and how
20 in his day we'd have been given 'six of the best', whatever that meant.

Just then, a car pulled up by the side of the road and a pretty woman with blonde hair wound down the window.

'You having a go at these kids?' she challenged the man. 'Leave them alone!'

25 She got out of the car and Kitty immediately flew to her side, wrapping her arms round her legs, whooping with excitement and shouting, 'Mummy! Mummy!'

---

1 **racket** loud unpleasant noise – 4 **disgust** feeling of very strong dislike – 12 **unholy** awful, appalling, horrible – 13 **savage** brutal or violent person – 13 **to play truant** *(idm)* to stay away from school without permission – 20 **six of the best** *(idm, old)* sechs Schläge *(mit dem Stock)*

The man tut-tutted and scurried away, all the fight gone out of him, muttering about 'bad parents' and 'kids these days'.

'Well he was a charmer, wasn't he? Hi, everyone. I'm Marie Harris. Kit and Rudy's mum, in case this little leg grabber hadn't already
5   made that obvious. How's it going?'

I couldn't help wishing my mum was like Rudy's. She didn't seem at all bothered about Rudy and Kitty not being in school. All she said to Rudy was to let her know next time he was taking Kitty off somewhere without telling her so she could let Kitty's school know.
10 They'd rung up in a panic after some other kid saw Kitty getting on the 'Big School' bus.

'Don't take me home!' pleaded Kitty. 'Don't take me to school! I won't go. This is Fridays for Future!'

Her mum smiled. 'Not going to, Kits. You carry right on. Proud
15 of you.'

She turned to Zaynab and me.

'This your idea? What's your strategy? Got the press lined up? Got any leaflets or anything to give people? Something they can do? An action they can take? Or are you just having a bit of fun?'
20 I could see Zaynab's temper beginning to flare, but before she could say anything, Mrs Harris carried on. 'Only I can call the local paper, if you want. Friend of mine is a journalist there and he'll come straight on over. Better have your story ready, though. What's your message?'
25 For a split second Zaynab looked blank and then an expression of frustration passed across her face.

We hadn't thought about the papers at all. Even worse, we had not really thought about what effect we wanted to have. Did that mean it was a failure?
30 'Or maybe ...' Mrs Harris was watching Zaynab's face carefully, 'maybe you'd be better keeping your powder dry.'

---

1 **to scurry away** to hurry away – 17 **to line up** *here:* to arrange to be there – 20 **temper** tendency to become angry quickly – 20 **to flare** to fire up, to burst out – 29 **failure** lack of success, defeat – 31 **to keep one's powder dry** *(idm)* to be prepared and hold back one's resources until they are needed in the future

Zaynab looked baffled.

'Sorry?'

'You know … wait until you have a really big turnout before getting the press involved. You don't want them to say it was a damp squib, do you? Mind you, that's not a bad crowd you've mustered.'

We'd been so focused on Mr Angry that we hadn't noticed that Izzy and about a dozen other people were now crowding the pavement.

Izzy smiled shyly.

'I know you thought I'd bailed,' she said, 'but not everyone takes the bus, you know. Anyway, I got these people to come, too.'

'I'm filming,' said Sophie-Ann. 'Want to say something to the camera, Zaynab?'

I would have been terrified if I'd been asked to speak, but Zaynab wasn't fazed at all.

'Today is our first protest and it is quite small, but it will grow and grow. We have been silent for too long. It is time to speak out. We want climate justice and we want it now. Join us.'

Sophie-Ann stuck her thumb up. 'Great! That'll go viral.'

'Wow!' said Kitty. 'You're just like Greta, only a different colour!' Mrs Harris hugged her.

'Every colour, every country, maybe even every city or town has their own Greta, Kits. Looks like we've got ours.'

But then Mrs Baldwin arrived and we all knew instantly that we were in deep doodoo.

'OK, everyone.' Mrs Baldwin clapped her hands to get our attention. 'Back to school straight away, please. All of you mini Rambos stay here for a moment. Yes, you with the face paint. Especially you, Aoife Coleman and you, Jack Kerrow. What a surprise! And Sophie-Ann! You seem to have forgotten the events of last year. How very convenient.'

---

1 **baffled** not understanding, confused – 4 **damp squib** *(idm)* an event that is much less impressive than expected *(Reinfall)* – 5 **to muster** to gather, collect – 15 **to be fazed** to be worried, concerned – 19 **viral** sth that spreads quickly because people share it on social media – 24 **instantly** immediately, at once – 25 **doodoo** *(inf) here:* trouble – 31 **convenient** suitable, fitting

Mrs Harris stepped forward to say something, but Mrs Baldwin cut her off. 'You'll be wanting to get your daughter back into school as soon as possible, Mrs Harris, I am sure.'

For a moment, I thought Kitty's mum was going to tell her where to get off, but she just smiled and said, 'They're good kids, you know. They're fighting for the right cause.'

'It may well be the right cause, but this is not the right way.'

Mrs Baldwin looked as if she was really finding it hard to be polite to Mrs Harris.

I was beginning to feel a bit sick. Dad would be beyond angry if I got suspended and Mum would be really disappointed in me, which was worse.

Zaynab stepped forward, eyes blazing in her eagle way.

'It wasn't Aoife's idea.'

'Really?' said Mrs Baldwin. 'We need a little talk, you and I. I'll see you at noon in my office. Now. Back to school, all of you, and for goodness' sake get that stuff off your faces. You look like something out of *Lord of the Flies*.'

So that was our first school strike for climate.

Could have gone better.

ZAYNAB

I suppose I was meant to feel terror as I waited outside Mrs Baldwin's door. Her secretary told me to sit down and wait until I was called, but I did not feel like doing that, so I walked up and down, looking at the school photographs going back to 1953. Three rows of kids
5 and teachers, smiling in the sunshine. Right up to 1999, there were some huge trees in the background but in 2000, they had gone and in 2003 there was a big building in their place which I recognised as the science labs.

The door opened and Mrs Baldwin beckoned me in.
10 'Sit down, Zaynab. And you can take that look off your face, I am on your side ... or more specifically, on the side of the environment.'

'On the side of the environment? You cut down the trees,' I said. 'You cut down all those beautiful trees for a building.'

I was still standing and wondering whether it was worth having
15 a conversation with this woman if she was going to lie to me from the start.

She frowned. 'Ah! Yes, well I am afraid those chestnuts were felled by my predecessor to make way for the science labs. He did plant a number of hardwoods over by the sports field. Now, why don't
20 you sit down? We need to talk.'

I sat down on the edge of the chair. I wanted to make it clear to her that I did not mean to stay a moment longer than was necessary.

'I find myself baffled by you, Zaynab. I am looking at the reports from your school. You're hardworking, polite, diligent. Quiet. Not
25 the sort of profile that would lead anyone to suspect that you might be a rebel and a revolutionary, and certainly not off your own bat, as it were. Quite the contrary. Yours is the profile of a model pupil.'

---

1 **terror** great fear – 9 **to beckon** to tell sb to come to them, to summon – 17 **chestnut** *Kastanie* – 18 **predecessor** ['priːdɪˌsesə] the person who had the job before – 19 **hardwoods** *Laubbäume* – 24 **diligent** hard-working, careful – 26 **off one's own bat** *(idm)* all alone, on one's own

I said nothing. I just stared at the pile of papers on her desk. The reports describing old Zaynab. Back home Zaynab. Solitary Zaynab.

'I know that you have been through a very great deal, Zaynab, and it cannot be easy being uprooted from all you know and "dumped", as it no doubt seems to you, in a strange place. The teachers here tell me that you seem to have settled down to working well and that you have been getting good marks. They were a little concerned that you were on your own a lot in the first week and that going off to pray would set you apart, but then you struck up your friendship with Lucas Rowe and we took that to be a very positive sign.'

I could tell without looking that she was hoping that I would say something. I wondered how many people really noticed my prayer absences, apart from Lucas, and why would it matter to them, anyway?

'Then something changed, didn't it? I cannot help feeling that you have come under the influence of other, older pupils.'

'Wrong,' I said.

'In what way "wrong"?' she asked, and I looked up at her. She was staring intently at me. I looked away again.

'They have come under *my* influence.'

'Are you saying that this morning's "event" was entirely your idea?'

'Yes.'

'Did Sophie-Ann not tell you that I had forbidden just such action last year?'

I nodded.

'And what about Aoife Coleman and Jack Kerrow?'

'Made the banner.'

'Hmm. Was that all they did?'

I nodded again.

She paused as if trying to work out what to say next. She seemed disappointed that I didn't want to put the blame on Aoife and Jack.

---

2 **solitary** unsociable, spending a lot of time alone – 4 **uprooted** removed – 5 **to dump** (*inf*) to abandon, leave

'Did it not occur to you that the school as a whole might want to participate in your little event? Might it not have been a good idea to discuss this with your class teacher?'

Was she trying to suggest that the school would have backed us going on strike? In the street, in public? More likely she'd have allowed it in class or in the playground at breaktime. Out of sight. Pointless!

'It would have been a different thing,' I replied. 'Anyway, if you cared, you should have been doing it already. It should not be left to a person like me to organise.'

She pursed her lips.

'It is not so simple, Zaynab. We have obligations and duties, no matter what our private views might be.'

'Well, there you go,' I said.

'But we could possibly have found a way to support your initiative. You would have had many more people involved, made a bigger impact and a bigger story, and all without breaking rules.'

'Making it a school thing would change it. I want people who care enough to just get up and do something. It's meaningless, otherwise,' I said.

'But if only the most passionate get involved, you risk having a very small group with very little influence. You have to take people with you, Zaynab. You are very young to be learning this lesson, but it is an important one. There is a phrase – "the lunatic fringe" – which is used to describe people who are extremists. I don't think you want to be part of that. Not if you really want to change the world.'

I did not want to hear her weak vision of the world and of people who cared.

'Why don't you feel scared?' I said. 'Why don't you feel desperate to do anything you can to stop the planet being destroyed? Why aren't we protesting every day? The Prophet, peace be upon him,

---

11 **to purse one's lips** to move them into a small, rounded shape because you disapprove of sth – 12 **obligation** responsibility, duty

said "The world is green and beautiful, and Allah has appointed you his guardian over it." We are failing.'

Mrs Baldwin sighed deeply.

'No matter what may or may not be happening to our environ-
5 ment, you do still need an education, Zaynab, and that is what we are under an obligation to provide.'

'An education for what? So that we can write about the death of the planet? So we can calculate how many days we have left? You aren't even telling the truth about what's actually happening.'

10 Mrs Baldwin took a deep breath.

'There is a balance to be struck, Zaynab. Climate change plays a big part in the curriculum, especially if you choose to do geography for your GCSEs.'

'But it should be in *everything*. Don't you get it? There are
15 countries that won't exist and people who will die if you adults keep on pretending that nothing is happening or that it's not as bad as it is.'

'We cannot frighten people, Zaynab. There is nothing to be gained by frightening people when there is nothing you can give them to
20 do with that fear. I cannot have a school filled with children too scared to sleep at night, too worried to eat or enjoy their childhood. The parents would not tolerate that, for a start.'

I didn't see why she should wriggle out of this by blaming the parents.

25 'You have to do something. It is your job,' I said, staring at her unflinchingly.

She sat back in her chair and closed her eyes. I could almost hear her counting to ten in her head.

'Very well. Here is my suggestion. Put a proposal to me about
30 how we could be doing more than we already do and we will consider whether to take up these proposals. I am not promising anything, but can we agree that this is a way forward?'

---

1 **to appoint** to choose sb for a certain job – 2 **guardian** sb who protects sth – 13 **GCSE** *abbr of* General Certificate of Secondary Education *(britische Schulabschlussprüfung)* – 26 **unflinchingly** steadily, determinedly – 29 **proposal** a written plan of ideas, suggestions

I grunted. Was she wasting my time? Our time? We'd have to see.
I got up to go.

'You won't suspend the others, will you?'

She gave me a stony look.

5   'I await your proposals, Zaynab. You stand out, Zaynab, for all
sorts of reasons, as I am sure you are only too aware. If I were you,
I would make sure I stood out for the right reasons.'

Her words echoed around my head for a long time. From her,
they were a kind of threat but maybe I could turn them into a
10 challenge.

LUCAS

Zaynab hadn't been able to tell me what the head had said because she missed lunchbreak. It can't have been bad, because none of us got into trouble, not even Aoife and Jack. I was very relieved because Dad would have gone nuts if I'd been suspended and there would
5 have been no way to keep the story from him if I had. Most of the inhabitants of Yewburton had either seen us or, like Mum, had heard all about it from the town's gossips when they came into the shop. Some had described us as a wild bunch of kids gone crazy, but others had said they were glad that young people cared. Mum didn't
10 say so, but I think she was actually secretly proud of me and she was just as keen as me to make sure that Dad did not find out.

Thank goodness Mrs Harris had never got that journalist to come round, I thought, and thank goodness Dad wasn't on TikTok or Facebook or he'd have seen Zaynab for sure. The video had had over
15 a thousand hits and been shared on the Yewburton Community page.

But I'd forgotten all about Mr Angry. He must have emailed the local paper the minute he got home, just in time for the Saturday edition. Just my luck!
20 'That foreign kid's been causing trouble, I see,' Dad said, holding out the paper for Mum to read, while he returned to his breakfast.

Mum went very pale but she took the paper and quickly read the letter before handing it back, saying, 'Mr Weatherstaff complains about everything. He's a nasty man. Always looking for things to
25 moan about.'

'Says there were lots of kids, dancing about like savages, skiving off school. Bloody disgrace. You know anything about this, Lucas?'

I pretended not to have been listening. He waved the paper at me.

---

3 **relieved** happy because sth unpleasant has not happened – 25 **to moan** to complain – 26 **to skive off** (inf) to stay away (from school) without permission

'Here. Read all about it.'

The letter was in bold with the headline: 'Local kids run wild.'

Mr Weatherstaff ranted on, describing us as hooligans, threatening him – a frail old man – blocking the road, intimidating passers-by.
5 He said the leader was a young girl 'very far from being local', so anyone who knew about Zaynab would know instantly what he meant by that. There was nothing about the reason for our protest. He was happy to let everyone think we were just playing truant.

I wanted to tell Dad what had actually happened, but Mum caught
10 my eye and gave me a look which told me, very clearly, 'Say nothing.'

Lara came down, still dressed in her bathrobe, and started rooting about in the fridge. She was just making a fat cheese toastie when she glanced down at the paper.

'Hey, kiddo! You making a splash?' She laughed.
15 I made a 'zip it' sign at her, pointing at Dad, who had finished his breakfast and was busy selecting fishhooks from a big box. Lara covered her mouth for a moment and then whispered, 'Sorry!'

'Who's making a splash?' Dad asked.

She answered quick as a flash, 'Lucas. At the swimming gala!'
20 I really, really love my sister, even when she gets me out of one situation and straight into another, like this time.

'Swimming gala? Never knew you was a star swimmer, Lucas? Thought you took after your old man, sinking like a stone.' He carried on with his selection, scattering stuff all over the table. 'Is there a
25 report in the paper, then?'

'No. I just thought there might be ...' Lara was making wild faces at me now and seemed on the brink of hysterical laughter.

Dad muttered something and then gathered up his kit and headed out, letting the backdoor slam shut behind him.
30 'Oh my God!' Lara dissolved into helpless giggles, snorting and spitting toast crumbs. Mum shook her head at her.

'Swimming gala! What on earth made you say that, Lara?'

---

3 **to rant** to speak loudly or angrily – 4 **frail** not very strong or healthy – 4 **to intimidate** to frighten or threaten sb – 14 **to make a splash** *(inf)* to attract a lot of attention

'Well, I thought it was quite smart of me to explain it that way, making a splash and all that!' Lara said, sniffily, picking crumbs off her robe. 'OK. But it was better than telling him that Lucas is bunking off school with an immigrant and getting the whole racist cliché
5 thing kicking off again.'

'Lara!' Mum's voice sounded cracked, tired.

'Yeah. OK. But you know what I mean. He's like so triggered by everything. It's beyond grim. What will he do when he finds out who Lucas's bestie is?'

10 'Doesn't need to know, does he? Anyway, she's not my bestie. That's ridiculous,' I said. Even as I said it, I felt I was letting Zaynab down. I should have wanted to tell the truth and stand up for her, but I knew that I wouldn't be the only one to have to suffer the fallout. When Dad lost his rag, everyone got a piece of the action.

15 Mum folded the newspaper away. 'He's not easy, I know. But he is your father. And he does love you.' She stuffed the paper in the recycling bag.

'Not easy? Woah. Understatement. Of. The. Decade.'

Mum stared pointedly at Lara, who had started eating marmalade
20 out of the jar. 'You're not that far off a cliché, yourself, Lara. Up late. Moody. Yes! Moody!'

'They've done research that proves people my age need way more sleep and should be allowed to stay in bed longer. In some European countries, they don't start school until ten or even eleven in the
25 morning. Not in this Stone-Age place, though, oh no. Anyway, I'm not even that late today. Not for a Saturday.'

Mum smiled. 'True. Not bad for a Saturday. Any reason?'

'Going to Plymouth. Meeting friends. Going to need some cash, though.'

30 She held out her hand.

'Pretty please.'

---

2 **sniffily** in an arrogant way – 7 **to trigger** to set off, to activate – 8 **grim** unpleasant, depressing – 13 **to suffer** *here*: to feel or experience – 14 **to lose one's rag** *(idm)* to suddenly become so angry that you are not in control of yourself – 14 **to get a piece of the action** *(idm) here*: to be affected

Mum sighed. 'You know, you could get some hours at the shop, if you wanted.'

'Ugh! As if! Thanks, Mum.' She gave Mum a quick kiss on the cheek as she rolled the ten-pound note up tightly.

5 'If Dad thinks I should get a job, you definitely should,' I found myself saying.

Lara fixed me with a stare. 'I think you need me on your side, bro, don't you?' Then she laughed and ruffled my hair. 'Only teasing, kiddo. Watch this space. Shower time! If you need the loo, better go 10 now!'

Our only toilet was in the bathroom. If Lara got in there first, it could be an utter disaster. She would be in there for weeks. Well, not weeks, but easily an hour. It drove Dad crazy.

But then nearly everything drove Dad crazy.

15 'What are you doing today, love?' Mum asked me. 'Have you shown your friend the moors? It's a beautiful day. Why don't you see if she'd like to walk up there with you?'

'Already planned to, once I've finished my chores,' I replied, starting to clear away the breakfast things.

20 'Leave them for now. Do them when you get back. This sun is only forecast to last until the afternoon. You make the most of it. Go on. You can take my boots for her, if you want. I doubt she has any and she's quite tall for a twelve-year-old, her feet might not be that much smaller than mine.'

25 I hugged her. Not something I did very often. She looked so happy. *I must hug her more often*, I thought, as I packed up my rucksack.

---

12 **utter** complete, absolute – 18 **chores** household tasks

ZAYNAB

I was not happy about my 'little chat' with Mrs Baldwin but at least she had not told my father about anything and he had not heard about our protest from anyone else. I was certain that I would have had a long lecture about manners and rules and obedience,
5 especially with him fresh back from Friday prayers.

If Mama had been alive, she would have wanted to hear all about it and she would have been proud. I could have told her about Mrs Baldwin and how she had made me feel and asked her what I should do to get rid of the anger. Mama would probably have demanded
10 to see Mrs B and told her just what she thought of her attempts to stop us protesting.

I could visualise their meeting in my head and it made me smile. Mama in tatty jeans, with her wild mane of hair and fierce green eyes, storming into the head's office, ready to go to war for me. Mrs
15 Baldwin would have been reduced to a jelly.

That was an 'if only'. A very big one.

I needed a distraction until Lucas arrived. I wandered out into Deborah's little garden, which was like an oasis in the middle of the bleakness of the moor. Even though winter was coming, it still had
20 plenty of colour. A beautiful climbing rose covered one wall and I was just about to go and smell the flowers when Deborah appeared.

'I've got a little microclimate in here,' she explained. 'The walls shelter us and retain the heat of the sun, at least that's my theory. That rose will flower until Christmas, with luck.'

25 I told her we did not celebrate Christmas and she apologised, saying she hadn't thought about that.

Deborah began cutting deadheads off the rose. She may have carried on talking to me, but I wasn't listening. My mind was with

---

4 **obedience** the act of obeying *(Gehorsam)* – 10 **attempt** try, effort – 13 **tatty** old and in a bad condition – 17 **distraction** act of keeping sb's concentration off sth – 19 **bleakness** looking cold and empty

Mama, back when I was really young. We had done Christmas things when we lived in Bristol, though I could not really remember them, because we had left when I was only four years old. Father had a picture of the three of us standing under a huge tree in a square
5   near the University when I was just a baby, all dressed up for winter. I found the picture in her drawer when I was helping her to sort out her things for her first time in hospital and I said, 'I look just like a Christmas present, all wrapped up.' Mama cried and held me tight and said I was the best present a mama could ever have.

10 That was something I sometimes wished I did not remember but, at the same time, it was something I hoped I would never ever forget.

Father came into the garden with a cup of coffee in one hand and a sheaf of papers in the other. Deborah went back into the cottage, leaving us alone.

15 'What are you doing today, Zaynab? I thought perhaps we might go for a walk, once I have finished some work.'

'Got plans,' I said, squeezing past him. As I brushed by, I caught the papers on my jumper and some of them fluttered into the flower beds and onto the gravel path, much to Father's annoyance.

20 'You're so clumsy, sometimes,' he said. 'Now they'll be in a muddle!'

I could not help glancing at the pages as I gathered them up from the flower bed. I could not read it quickly enough, but some words jumped out.

25 *Feasibility Study: Jurassic Oil and Gas. Relocation of nomadic peoples. Replanting programme.*

I must have found it hard to hide my disgust as I handed the papers to Father.

'You are angry because I'm working with an oil company,' he said.
30 'You assume the worst. Everyone does.' He lifted my chin with his hand so that he could look straight at me. 'We cannot change the world by turning our backs on these companies. We must help

---

19 **gravel** very small stones – 19 **annoyance** feeling you get when sb makes you angry – 20 **clumsy** to handle things carelessly – 25 **feasibility** sth that can be done, made or achieved – 30 **to assume** to guess

them to change and evolve and to act as stewards of the land, as the Prophet, blessings be upon him, commanded. That is the sustainable way.'

'Sustainable way for them to carry on making money, you mean?' I said, angrily. 'What would Mama have said? What would she have done? She'd have stood up to them, not helped them!'

A shadow passed over his face.

'I am sure things all look very simple to you. Cut and dried. Black and white. If only it were that easy. Your mama understood even things done with the best of intentions can have unforeseen consequences and not every dramatic action produces dramatic results. Not that she let that stop her.'

'Are you saying she wasted her time?' I snapped.

He sighed. 'We need to talk, you and I.'

I heard the front door open and Deborah chatting away to Lucas. 'I have to go,' I said.

'Fine.' He looked relieved. Then he added, 'I must say that it is good to see you making friends. You seem to be settling in very well.'

'I'm not settling in,' I said. 'I'm taking over.'

And before I could hear his reaction to that, I darted back into the house, to find my friend smiling broadly and holding out a pair of walking boots for me.

---

1 **steward** a person who manages sth – 3 **sustainable** describes the steady use of resources at a level that does not damage the environment – 18 **to settle in** to become used to living in a new place – 20 **to dart** to run, to race

LUCAS

It took me nearly an hour to walk up the steep hill that led out of
our hamlet onto the moors and then along the winding road, over
another cattle grid and down a sharp dip to the stony track which
led to Hope Cottage. I really looked at it this time. Last time I'd
5 visited, Zaynab had run all the way down the private track and we
had piled into the house before I had time to take it all in. Hope
Cottage stood alone on the left, with a little stone-walled garden all
around it. Two flags were flying, a rainbow and an EU flag, both
quite tattered from the wind. Opposite was a long farmhouse which
10 seemed to be deserted. Many of the windows were broken and the
front door hung off its hinges. The huge haybarn was full, though,
with massive rolls of hay, much, much taller than me.

The moorland beyond the barn was divided into fields with a
mixture of tumbled down walls and barbed wire. Clumps of wool
15 stuck to the lower strands of wire where sheep had decided that the
grass was greener and had tried to wriggle through. Bit crazy really,
because the grass was all the same – cropped right down as if it had
been mown and then littered with stones and boulders.

There were two ponies in the nearest field, eating from a pile of
20 hay thrown out near the gate. A mare and her foal. She was a rich
brown. The foal was nearly black and getting a very woolly coat,
ready for winter. The foal stopped eating to look at me for a moment
and I forgot about knocking on the cottage door and reached for
one of the apples in my pocket.

25 'Don't feed it,' a voice behind me said.

I turned round to see Mrs Wonnacott, Deborah, coming out of
her front door.

---

9 **tattered** damaged, torn – 11 **haybarn** *Heuscheune* – 14 **barbed wire** strong wire with
sharp points used to make fences – 18 **to mow (mowed, mown)** to cut grass –
18 **boulder** large rounded rock *(Felsbrocken, Geröll)*

'It's terribly tempting, I know, but you, as a local, should know about not feeding the ponies.' She didn't say this unkindly.

'I thought an apple would be OK,' I replied, stuffing it back into my pocket.

5 'Well, it probably would, but then you have begun to teach that little fellow that humans bring treats and then he'll be offered all sorts of stuff by tourists. You should see the rubbish they try to feed them! Scones. Ice cream. Crisps. Someone tipped a whole box of windfalls out at the bottom of Rippon Tor and the ponies binged

10 out. At least two had to be treated for colic ... a kind of severe stomach ache which can be fatal. So, it's best not to. Have you come for Zaynab? Come in. Have a drink and a biscuit.'

We had just got in the door when Zaynab appeared. She seemed to be in a huge hurry to get going, grabbing the boots and sitting

15 down on the stairs to put them on.

She had them on in seconds and, grabbing her coat, she made for the door.

'Zaynab! Wait one moment, please.'

Her dad came into the hall.

20 I knew that I liked him the minute I saw him, just like I had with Zaynab.

He was tall and dark with a small beard and moustache and a big, warm smile. He held out his hand.

'Professor Egal, but you may call me sir.' He laughed and ruffled

25 my hair. 'Only joking. I'm Zaynab's papa. You can call me Liban. And you are?'

Hadn't Zaynab ever mentioned me?

He smiled and continued, 'You see, I am afraid my darling daughter tells her poor old father nothing about her life. Maybe you

30 can fill me in on what she's been up to?'

'I'm Lucas. Lucas Rowe. I don't really want to be a spy, sir.'

The professor laughed again.

---

6 **treat** a special item of food *(Leckerbissen)* – 8 **scone** a small cake usually eaten with butter and jam – 9 **windfall** fruit that has fallen from a tree – 11 **fatal** deadly – 31 **spy** secret agent

'Of course you don't. So, where are you off to?'

'Out,' said Zaynab, waiting in the doorway with her back turned. That was one thing about Zaynab. When she was in a mood with you, you knew all about it.

5 'I'd love a walk on the moors, too. Lucas, are you our go-to guide?'

'He's not a guide. He's my friend. Go on your own walk ... when you have finished your important work.' Zaynab's voice was icy cold.

'Of course, Of course.' He tried to laugh it off. 'Zaynab's right. I have a lot of work to do.' He patted the bundle of papers. 'But I'll 10 be happy to take you both out if you are back in time for lunch. We could walk to the café at the farm shop down the road. And you, too, of course, Deborah. If you would like to join us. How about that? It would be nice to talk to you, Lucas, and I promise not to interrogate you about Zaynab.'

15 'Not happening,' Zaynab cut in. 'Lucas and I have other plans.'

'Well, let me at least give you some money.'

He held out a ten-pound note.

She snatched it, muttered thanks, I think, and set off down the track beyond the farmhouse. She seemed to be travelling at about 20 a million miles an hour.

'What is it with you and your dad?' I asked when I caught up with her.

'I hate him,' she said, and started off again.

'I'm not that keen on mine. And you'd know why the minute you 25 met him. But your dad ... your dad seems really nice, I mean, really.'

'Yeah, well "seems" and "is" are two totally different things, aren't they, or haven't you discovered that yet?'

I pulled on her coat to stop her from going further.

'I don't want to talk about it,' she said, tucking her hair back under 30 her headscarf.

'That's fine. But you're going the wrong way. We'll have to go back past the cottage.'

14 **to interrogate** to question

'Oh.' She turned round and I could see she had been crying. I decided it was best to pretend I hadn't noticed. We said nothing as we passed the gate and headed up towards the road.

'There was a letter about us in the paper today. That angry man.
5 Not very nice. My dad saw it. Lara nearly told him I was there.'

'Why wouldn't you tell him? You should be proud about it,' she said, kicking a stone into a puddle.

'I know. But, like I said, if you met my dad ... Anyway, you haven't told your dad, have you?'

10 She didn't reply. We walked in silence for a while. I wanted to show her the view from Rippon Tor. Most tourists went up Haytor Rocks so it got really crowded pretty much any time the sun came out. I liked Rippon because you got really good three-hundred-and-sixty-degree views and you could see all the way to the Teign Estuary
15 and the sea and Fernworthy Forest and as far as Princetown on a clear day. Best of all, almost no one went up it except local people. There was a triangulation pillar as well, which was interesting to some people. Not me, particularly.

We climbed steadily, picking our way over the tussocks of grass
20 and boulders, some of them slimy or covered with bright green moss. The turf was springy beneath our feet, saturated with water, the black, peaty soil like a sponge.

'We're probably killing lots of stuff by walking on it,' Zaynab said, gloomily.

25 'Or maybe spreading it further?' I said. 'Helping plants meet new plants!'

'You aren't going to convince me that it's good for them.' Zaynab seemed determined to stay cross.

A group of sheep stood in our path for a while, their jaws grinding
30 sideways. We moved to go round them, but they skipped off down the hillside a short way.

'No one looks after these sheep?' Zaynab asked, in surprise.

---

17 **triangulation pillar** *Vermessungssäule* – 19 **steadily** without stopping – 19 **tussock**
Büschel – 21 **turf** *Torf* – 21 **saturated** extremely wet, soaked – 22 **peaty soil**
Moorboden – 24 **gloomy** unhappy – 28 **cross** annoyed

'There's nothing here that will kill them once they are big like these. A fox will take lambs, but once they're fully grown, I think they are safe from anything. Apart from the Beast of Bodmin, only this isn't Bodmin. People do say they've seen a beast here, though.
A big cat. Maybe someone's pet leopard or puma. You know, some rich person's-'

'It would be a cheetah, in my country,' Zaynab interrupted, 'though smugglers have taken many away to be pets in the palaces in the Gulf. Most of them die before they even get to Saudi or Kuwait, but if they make it, their rich owners take pictures of them, sitting in their golden gas-guzzling trucks, wearing diamond-studded collars. It's disgusting.'

'Maybe the beast is one of those cheetahs. Wouldn't that be amazing?'

'Unbelievable. Literally.' She looked at me as if to say 'you're an idiot', and then she was off again at her fast pace.

She was stomping. That was the only way to describe it. I was just thinking about how much you could tell about a person's mood from how they were walking or even sitting and how Dad sat with his legs wide apart while Mum sat with hers crossed (almost twice, with the toes of one foot behind the other calf, making herself very small) when Zaynab stopped to speak again: 'Many of the sheep in my country have died. The herders take them in search of water, but there is none. So they just die. The herders, too, sometimes. Were there trees here once?'

'Thousands of years ago. It used to be warmer, actually, in the Bronze Age. Men came and started felling the trees and clearing the land by burning.'

'Some things never change.'

'People used to cut peat turves to burn in the winter. Dad said my great-grandfather used to make a living from it. He gets very angry that it was stopped because it's bad for the environment. He's not big on being green.'

7 **cheetah** large wild cat that can run very fast *(Gepard)* – 12 **collar** *here:* a band which is put around the neck of an animal

'What is peat, anyway?' Zaynab asked, as we climbed.

'It's what's left of ancient plants and woods, buried for millions of years. It's basically a store of carbon, from the trees that grew in the sun all that time ago. Dad said his grandad used to say that burning peat's like burning sunlight. He was right, if you think about it. Same as coal and oil or any fossil fuel.'

We were nearly at the top. I let Zaynab go first. I felt it was important for her to go in front of me. I couldn't say why.

She walked around the largest of the three heaps of rock and then sat down, looking out towards Fernworthy Forest.

'Maybe all the trees will come back when we have gone. When the sun has burned us up instead of us burning sunlight.'

I felt a little zing of pride that she had used my great-grandad's phrase. I didn't think she'd been listening.

I climbed higher up and looked round at the moors, stretched out for miles. I tried to imagine it covered in trees.

'They've burned nearly all the trees in parts of my country,' Zaynab continued, her voice almost too faint for me to hear. I climbed down to sit next to her. 'Made them into charcoal and sent them away to China. It's illegal, but they still do it.'

'Aren't there any trees at all? I had a look on Google and it looked like there were quite a lot in some places and green fields. It looked beautiful.'

'Ha! You have seen pictures for tourists. It is true we have some trees and fields of green, in Borama. We are lucky. But my country is trapped between the desert and the sea, and the desert is growing. In the drought regions, there are some trees that have grown by themselves. Want to know what the old people call them?'

I nodded.

'The Don't Know trees, because no one knows what they are. How sad is that?'

18 **faint** weak – 26 **trapped** caught in an unpleasant situation that is difficult to escape from

I didn't know what to say. Zaynab looked as if she was very far away. Maybe she was feeling homesick. I decided to change the subject.

'What did Mrs Baldwin say?'

5   Zaynab sighed and picked at a clump of heather absentmindedly.

'That we should have got her permission. That we would have had more people if the school had known and she had organised it.'

'Wow!'

10   Zaynab frowned. 'What is "wow" about it?'

'Well, you've already changed things. If Mrs B helps, the next protest will be way bigger.'

Zaynab slid down from the rock.

'She just wants to muscle in and get some credit. And now we
15   have to tell her what else we want the school to do and she may not even agree do it. I could tell she did not really care about any of it at all. She just wants to get some glory for her precious school. Make herself look good. It will probably get her a better job or more money, or something.'

20   I was confused. Surely Zaynab wanted the school to do more? Why was she so cross that Mrs Baldwin wanted to get involved? Did it matter what her reasons were?

'Sounds like a result, to me. Can I help you with the ideas?'

'Sure. Can we go and get something to eat now, Lucas? Might as
25   well spend this.' She fished the note out of her pocket. 'He only gave it to us to show off to you. That is why he invited you to lunch.'

Chances of my dad giving me a tenner or asking anyone to lunch? Zero.

'I still think your dad is nicer than mine,' I said, as we semi ran,
30   semi jumped down the slope.

'You do not know him,' was all she said.

---

5 **heather** *Heidekraut* – 14 **to get credit** to get praise and honour – 30 **slope** side of a mountain

ZAYNAB

We had walked so far from Deborah's cottage towards Yewburton
that we could not have got back to eat with father even if I had
wanted to. It was Lucas's idea to go to a café which he said had
Extinction Rebellion posters up in its window, but then he nearly
5   chickened out.

'This was a stupid idea. We can't afford this. I mean, *I* can't. They
won't serve kids without parents,' he said, when we got to Rafikis'
bright orange building.

We looked in through the steamed-up windows. It was full of
10   people eating and talking and looking happy. I suddenly felt my
energy and excitement returning.

'We have to go in. This is where we are meant to be,' I said. 'Look
… the portions are huge. I just know that they will let us share. And
I am paying.'

15   The scent of spices filled the small, steamy, warm room. The long
benches were heaped with beautiful cushions in African prints and
there were posters of the Atlas Mountains, the Sahara and Petra on
the walls.

No one seemed to mind that we were children. The women in
20   the kitchen waved at us as if they knew us well.

'Sit! Sit!' they cried, all smiles.

I felt so homesick right then. They were not my people. They were
ordinary English women, but they were warm and welcoming in a
way that so many English were not.

25   Lucas was nervous.

'Stop worrying. Look around you,' I said. 'These are good people
and this is a good place.'

'I'll just be a minute,' he said and disappeared through a door at
the back. When he returned, he had a huge smile on his face.

---

6 **to afford sth** to have enough money to pay for sth – 15 **scent** smell

'The toilet is twinned! Twinned with a toilet in Ethiopia! There's a picture of the one Rafikis have paid for in a village. What a brilliant idea!'

'Ethiopia is our next-door neighbour!' I said. 'I told you this was
5 a good place.'

'Why do you always know more about everything than me?' Lucas asked. 'I mean, it's embarrassing. I've lived here all my life and never been in this café or heard about toilet twinning. Hey! That's something the school could do!'

10 I shook my head. 'No. Not now. We must stay focused. Climate emergency.'

He looked disappointed.

'If we don't stop what's happening to the planet, there won't *be* any toilets in Africa.'

15 One of the women came over.

'We saw you out protesting. Fantastic. Really amazing. You're up at Deborah's, aren't you? Is she helping you?'

I felt a little fizzle of anger. Why did everyone always assume we needed help?

20 'No. We are doing this ourselves. It's our future. We are the ones who must fight for it.'

'Fair play,' she said. 'But we oldies will be doing our thing, too. We aren't all the enemy. I'm Cath, by the way. And you're Megan's boy, aren't you?'

25 Lucas nodded, shyly.

'Great! So we're all friends! Now. What would you like?'

I felt bad. I didn't need to give every adult a hard time. She was obviously really kind and good.

I studied the menu. There was a spicy stew of black-eyed peas,
30 sweet potato and peanuts which sounded perfect. Not quite what we ate at home, but near enough.

'Can we have that, please? It sounds really wonderful. With two spoons?'

23 **enemy** sb who is against you

Cath smiled broadly. 'It's got Scotch Bonnet chillies in it. Quite fiery! Think you can cope?'

I know I rolled my eyes as I replied, 'Give me food that tastes of something, please!'

5 She brought us a huge bowl. The stew was a gorgeous mix of colours and textures and I breathed in the steam.

'On the house. Last of today's batch, so you are doing us a favour,' Cath said, as she set it down between us and gave us each a smaller bowl and spoon. 'Enjoy!'

10 I said 'Jazakallah,' and noticed Lucas mutter it, too, flushing scarlet as he did so. I focused on the food as if I had not heard or seen him. He got embarrassed really easily.

It was so, so good. I ate with my eyes closed and suddenly I was beside a campfire with Mama, a baby in my lap, watching as the
15 women ladled out food for the circle of hungry children.

When I finally put my spoon down, I realised Lucas was watching me intently.

'You must get homesick,' he said, quietly. 'Do you miss your friends?'

20 I frowned. 'No. I do not really have friends. Not good friends, anyway. It was really just Mama and me.'

'What did you mean about your dad?' he asked.

I looked away. I didn't want to talk about him right then.

'Is it because he's doing work with an oil company?' Lucas
25 persisted.

'That, and a whole load of other stuff.' I changed the subject. 'We need to plan what we are going to do next.'

'We've got to give Mrs Baldwin some ideas, haven't we? We could start there. I think it's good that she wants to help, really, I do.'

30 'And if she doesn't agree to our suggestions?'

'Well. We should try and do them, anyway.' A defiant look came over his face.

---

2 **fiery** spicy, hot – 7 **batch** *here:* the amount produced in one cooking session –
10 **scarlet** bright red – 30 **suggestion** idea or plan that sb puts forward – 31 **defiant** rebellious

Lucas was so trusting, so optimistic. I felt a sudden rush of warmth towards him.

We started making a list and Lucas came up with lots of things we could be doing – a daily climate change bulletin in assembly,
5 an online newspaper, a campaign poster competition ... which he would win, I told him. It was fun and the time flew by.

'I meant it about not having friends,' I said, when we had run out of ideas. 'Until now. I think you are my first real friend after Mama.'

'Same here. I mean you're my first real friend, too,' he said, looking
10 embarrassed and happy at the same time. 'Strange how things happen, isn't it?'

He was right. It was strange.

4 **assembly** gathering of all the teachers and the students at the beginning of a school day

ZAYNAB

'There's a big Climate Strike rally planned in Exeter next month. My mum's going, and everyone who is worried about the environment will be there – XR, the Greens, Greenpeace. Everyone. It will be massive,' Rudy told us, over our lunchtime meeting. 'I reckon Mrs
5 B will try to stop us if we go on strike again this Friday. Mum says we need to pick our battles, not fight everything.'

His mum had a point, but we would be missing four Fridays and that did not feel right. Mrs Baldwin might assume we had given up. Rudy seemed to sense my worries.
10 'It's a big deal. They get two or three thousand people there and the media *have* to cover it. Last time, they made the County Council agree to build more cycle lanes and before that they even persuaded them to declare a climate emergency and a target of being carbon neutral in eight years instead of twenty.'
15 'That is all very good,' I said, 'but we have just started our Fridays for Future campaign and we need to keep it going or it will fade away. We are just about to ask Mrs Baldwin to approve a demo every week. What will she think if we do not do that?'

Rudy nodded. 'I know where you are coming from, but trust me.
20 The focus for this rally is on investing more money in public transport to get cars off the road and reduce emissions and to stop the Council investing its pension fund in fossil fuel companies. It's perfect for us, for you. I really think we should put everything into it. Really.'
25 'And we pick up Fridays for Future again afterwards?' I asked.

'Of course,' Rudy agreed. 'What does everyone else think?'

'I vote we skip the next few Fridays and go for the big one,' said Aoife. 'Just go. How can she stop us?'

---

4 **to reckon** *(inf)* to think, to believe – 13 **to declare a climate emergency** *einen Klimanotstand verkünden* – 13 **target** a result that you are trying to achieve, goal – 21 **emission** *(usu pl)* release of gases into the atmosphere – 22 **pension fund** a fund of money that is used to pay people's pension

'We should get everyone to ask their parents for permission to go,' Izzy suggested. 'I'll make some reply slips.'

'Good idea,' agreed Sophie-Ann. 'It'll be like a petition. The more people who want to go, the harder Mrs B will find it to say no.'

5 She was right. We needed to outmanoeuvre Mrs Baldwin, but first I had to get our list of ideas to her. I had a feeling they would go straight in the bin if I waited, so, as soon as the meeting was over, Lucas and I went and slipped the envelope with our ideas in under her door. Lucas had suggested that we make a copy and give it to 10 Mr Reeves, so we dropped that off at the staffroom on our way back.

'Just in case,' Lucas said, as we headed back for class. 'You know what she's like.'

We spent every breaktime for the next two days telling people about the big Climate Strike and handing out the permission 15 requests Izzy had created. I was asked over and over about what it was like in Somaliland and I told them about the droughts, the great cyclone which had destroyed whole villages, the dead animals, the emergency camps and the way the desert was gradually taking over and how that would all just keep speeding up unless the West cut 20 its carbon emissions. I told them about little Faduma hugging my legs and whooping with joy when Mama and her charity's team fixed for her to go to school. I asked them if they could walk for eight days in search of water like eight-year-old Asha and six-year-old Halima, who arrived at the camp almost dead from dehydration.

25 When I told these stories, I just could not stop myself from crying. Who was looking after them now? Were Adia and Kesia, Mama's two main teammates, able to cope? Just thinking about it made me all the more determined to get people signed up. It was the only way I could help.

30 Everyone I spoke to promised to come. How could Mrs Baldwin refuse us now?

---

3 **petition** document signed by a lot of people to change sth – 5 **to outmanoeuvre** to outdo, to gain an advantage over sb – 17 **cyclone** violent tropical storm – 20 **carbon emissions** (pl) CO_2-Ausstoß – 24 **dehydration** condition of not having drunk enough water – 27 **to cope** to deal with a problem or situation

The next day, she caught up with Lucas and me on our way to science. I had never seen anyone look angrier.

'My office! Zaynab only. Not you, Lucas. Get to your class!'

Lucas looked terrified. I smiled at him to reassure him, but I felt
5   sick, too, as I followed the head to her office.

Her desk was piled high. I felt a little thrill of excitement and fear. Permission slips for the climate rally, lots of them.

She waved to me to sit down as she pushed the slips to one side.

'You're an interesting child, Zaynab. You're getting quite a
10 following. Even the little anarchists – you know what an anarchist is?'

I nodded and pulled my hijab more tightly round my head as if it would protect me from her bad energy.

'Even the little anarchists like Aoife seem to defer to you. It's
15 impressive.'

She paused and fished out our list from amongst the letters. She waved the piece of paper at me.

'And you're full of ideas, apparently, and entirely resistant to promoting them through the proper channels.'

20   'I do not really know what you mean,' I said, though I sort of did.

'Leaving aside for a moment your disregard for procedure, I am more than a little concerned about some of the stories that are going around, stories that are worrying pupils and parents or creating problems for the school – like these.' She tapped the pile of letters.
25 'I am sure you know what these are.'

I nodded and couldn't stop myself from grinning.

'I am not sure exactly what it is you want to achieve? I have told you before that I do not like creating fear and misery for its own sake.'

30   I sighed with frustration. We had been through all this before.

'I repeat: what exactly do you hope to achieve? I am inclined to think that this –' she pointed at the slips – 'is all rather more about

---

4 **to reassure** to make sb feel less worried – 14 **to defer** to accept sb's opinion because you respect them – 27 **to achieve** to accomplish, to fulfil, to reach – 31 **to be inclined to think** to be of the opinion

a little girl who likes to be the centre of attention, rather than anything to do with saving the planet from climate change.'

I gasped in disbelief. It was nothing like that. Nothing at all! What was she talking about?

5 'You have persisted in going behind the school's back to achieve your little revolution. You've been telling people about the terrible things that you say have been happening in your country to get them to sign up for your little demonstration. Frightening them with stories of floods, droughts, starvation. But have you been in danger
10 from a flood or starvation? You, personally?'

I shook my head.

'No. No, but I have seen stuff. I have been to the camps with my mama and the charity she worked for ...'

She ignored me.

15 'In fact, you live a rather privileged life, don't you? A more privileged life than, say, Lucas?'

I glared at her. 'What do you mean?'

'Well, you have been able to travel here, haven't you? I doubt Lucas will ever get on a plane. He may never even have a passport,
20 whereas you are fortunate to have one from the UK, or you wouldn't be permitted here, would you? And you don't live in the desert, in a hut with no water or electricity, do you? In fact, I looked up your city on the Internet, and it's all rather lush, isn't it?'

I nodded. I felt sick.

25 'So, I do not think it is very honest to paint a picture of poverty and suffering in order to get people to support you. Do you?'

'But I haven't–' I began, but she interrupted me.

'And I don't think your country would be at all happy to be portrayed that way, either. It's rather insulting, don't you think?'

30 I took a deep breath. 'I have not made up anything. We have had droughts, many, many droughts. We used to give them names, but now there are so many that we have stopped. Cattle and sheep have died and people have died. That's all true.'

9 **starvation** extreme suffering or death because there is no food – 20 **fortunate** lucky – 29 **insulting** rude or offensive

She just looked at me, coldly.

'And you don't have to be a victim to want to change things. You just have to care and want to do Allah's bidding,' I added.

'Ah. *Change* things. Well, that's it, isn't it? Do you really think you can change things? Anything?'

She smiled at me, but not in a nice way at all.

'Why are you so negative?' I said, angrily. 'If people change what they do in even a small way, it helps. If they use their cars less, if they eat less meat, if they turn off lights, mend clothes ... it all helps.'

'Many families here are already forced to do these things because of their own circumstances. It is fine for the likes of Poppy and Daisy Ellis, for example, to boast of their eco-credentials. But have you thought about how you might be making many children feel guilty that they cannot do more?'

She stood up and leaned across her desk, bringing her face very close to mine. I tried to hold her gaze and to stay strong, but she just glared at me harder and harder.

And then I cracked. I felt completely helpless. I burst into tears.

She sat down again and watched me sobbing for a while before passing me a tissue.

I blew my nose, noisily.

Mrs Baldwin said, very coldly and deliberately, 'I care as much about the future of our planet as you do, believe me.'

I didn't believe her. Not for one second.

'But I will not have you disrupting people's education. And I will not have scaremongering. You may wish to model yourself on Greta Thunberg, and run around telling everyone they should be panicking, but I won't have it. You're only here for six months, Zaynab. I think you should concentrate on your studies, rather than persuading children that their time is better spent on the streets of Exeter instead of in class, where they belong.'

---

18 **to crack** *here*: to lose control of one's emotions and actions – 20 **tissue** *Taschentuch* – 22 **deliberately** carefully and with a purpose – 26 **scaremongering** [ˈskeəˌmʌŋgərɪŋ] to accuse sb of deliberately spreading worrying stories to frighten people

She picked up the pile of slips and threw them in the bin.

'*I* will decide whether we participate in any of these media stunts. Not you. You may go. Miss Knox will be wondering where you have got to.'

5   'What about our ideas?' I said, feeling a tiny scrap of courage return.

Her eyes glinted.

'I have left Mr Reeves to review your suggestions and then I will make the final decision. He seems to have seen them already, so it
10 should not take too long. Run along. You have taken up quite enough of my time as it is.'

I didn't make it to Miss Knox's class. I sat in the girls' cloakroom for a while.

Gradually, I felt my anger and fight returning. When I emerged,
15 I bumped into the school secretary.

'You're creating quite a stir, I hear,' said Mrs Webber. 'It's good to see young people getting interested and tearing themselves away from their phones. We've been snowed under by parents' letters on that strike in Exeter. Never seen anything like it!'

20 'Mrs Baldwin won't allow it,' I said, sniffing.

'Oh, her. She'll come round. Her bark's worse than her bite.' Mrs Webber smiled. 'Besides, I know most of the teaching staff are right behind you! Keep going, dear! Just get back on the right side of her. You'll be fine.'

25 I felt sick at the thought of trying to get back on her right side. Did she even have one?

On the bus, I told the others what had happened.

'She's a freakin' fruit loop!' said Aoife. 'What a cow!'

'It's great that lots of teachers are on our side, though,' Lucas said.

30 'Of course they are!' Aoife stood up and shouted down the length of the bus, 'We are on the right side of history!'

---

2 **stunt** sth that is done in order to get publicity and attract attention – 7 **to glint** to gleam, to flash – 16 **stir** great excitement, sensation – 21 **sb's bark is worse than their bite** (*idm*) sb seems much more unfriendly than they really are

'She's picking on you because she's afraid of you,' Rudy said. 'She's a bully.'

'But why is she picking on Zaynab and not going for the rest of us?' Lucas asked.

5 Rudy shrugged. 'Because she knows that Zaynab has started something she can't control? Because it doesn't matter how hard she is on her, as she'll be going back home? I don't know. She's twisted, that's for sure.'

'She can't handle anyone who takes a stand,' Aoife said. 'That's
10 why she hates me, too. Not as much as she hates you, Zaynab, obvs.'

'Can we stop talking about Mrs B, now?' I said, remembering her last words to me. 'She's had quite enough of *my* time.'

Everyone laughed and I felt lighter and happier in my soul.

'Mum says the Red Rebel Brigade may come to the rally! They
15 appear all over the country. They're dead famous!' Rudy added, 'Look. They're all in red to represent the blood shared by all species. Mum saw them in Bristol and she says she'll never ever forget the experience.'

He showed us a video on his phone of a group of men and women
20 dressed in red flowing robes, with red cloth draped over their heads and round their eerie, white-painted faces. They looked beautiful and terrifying at the same time.

They moved very slowly, very gracefully through the crowds, as if they were just one creature, their faces totally blank, saying
25 nothing, hands stretched out as if they were asking for help or showing that they carried no weapons. It was incredible. It made me want to cry and when I looked round at the others, I could see that they felt the same way.

I hoped with all my heart that they would be there, with us.

---

8 **twisted** *here:* evil, sick – 10 **obvs** (*inf*) *abbr of* obviously – 15 **dead** *here:* very –
23 **gracefully** in a smooth and controlled way – 26 **incredible** unbelievable

ZAYNAB

I did not think I would get to sleep that night, but I actually did the moment my head touched the pillow.

I dreamed about the Red Rebel Brigade. I was in somewhere that was like the desert, but not, and a sandstorm blew up and they came out of the whirling cloud of sand. Their blood red robes billowed in the wind, their ghostly faces staring straight through me, reaching out to me, but never quite touching me.

Suddenly, one of them came right up to me, the white make-up on his (or maybe it was her?) face caked and cracking like salt from the sea, dried by the sun. Slowly the figure changed and turned into Mrs Baldwin.

I woke up with a jolt. I was crying. I felt strange, as if I had been on another planet with those weird, wonderful people, until Mrs Baldwin had ruined it all.

I lay in the dark for a while.

I checked my phone. 5:30am. Another two hours before I had to get up. I usually timed my routine so that when I went downstairs for breakfast, Father had already left to walk up the track to meet his work colleague and travel with him to the University.

'Are you trying to avoid your father, Zaynab, as well as me?' Deborah had said when she caught me hanging about upstairs one day when he was running late again, waiting for him to go.

'I don't know what you mean,' I had said. But I did.

Right now, I didn't want to think about my father or about Mama. I wanted to think about the dream.

I got up, pulled on my jeans, a big sweater and my headscarf and crept downstairs. I had worked out where the creakiest floorboards were and I managed to get all the way down without making a noise.

12 **jolt** an emotional shock

Moonlight streamed through the dusty panes of the kitchen window. Toffee was asleep on a pile of towels on the kitchen table. He was snoring.

I put on Lucas's mum's boots, grabbed my coat and opened the
5   front door. Cold air began to creep in.

I felt something brush my legs. Toffee had woken up and was at my feet.

'You can't come with me,' I whispered to him, but he just stared at me with his big green eyes and wriggled past my legs and out
10 onto the track.

'Grrrr,' I said. 'You aren't a dog. You can't go for a walk! Stay here.'

I set off up the track. It was as if I had stepped into a black-and-white film. Even Toffee looked grey in the moonlight. He seemed determined to join me, running ahead for a few paces, then
15 stopping, looking back and running on some more.

It was completely quiet. Above me there was a sky as starry as any I had ever seen in the desert. Different stars. I stopped to stare up at them and I could almost see them swirling, as if the sky was moving and I was fixed on the earth and very, very tiny. I felt dizzy.

20 I decided to walk towards Haytor. I could follow the road, which was lit like a silver river, winding up and down. Toffee was no longer close by. I turned back and saw him sitting on the rock at the end of Deborah's track.

'Wait for me,' I told him, but he jumped down and set off for home
25 and warmth.

I hadn't chosen to start fighting against climate change. Something had just made me feel that I had to do it: Mama. Being close to Mama.

I hadn't made myself leader. The others had. Or had they just let
30 me be, because I seemed to want to be in charge?

It wasn't about me.

But why had I felt so angry when Mrs Baldwin had wanted to take over Fridays for Future?

---

1 **dusty** *staubig* – 1 **pane** flat sheet of glass – 16 **starry** when many stars can be seen – 19 **dizzy** feeling that you are losing balance

Because I knew she did not mean it. I knew she was only pretending to care.

And now I knew she would try to stop everything we wanted to do. She'd happily stop us going to the Climate Strike.

5   I thought about the Red Rebels. What were they trying to tell me?

I found myself at the bottom of Saddle Tor. It was quite easy to get up to the rocks at the top, even with only the moonlight to see by.

It was bitterly cold and I felt my face going numb and my fingers
10   losing feeling, but I didn't mind.

I climbed onto the smaller, flatter heap of boulders, which were covered in grass and moss.

I lay back and stared up at the stars again. I must have fallen asleep because I woke, shivering, teeth chattering just as the sky
15   began to turn red. I knelt on rock to perform Fajr, the dawn prayer.

Then I checked my phone. 07:15 am.

Fifteen minutes to get back and into my room. Past Dad having breakfast.

Impossible.

20   Unless. Unless, I cut down the steep side and across the fields. I was sure I'd find gates in the stone walls or could get through the gaps where they had fallen down.

Before I could stop myself, I was descending quite fast, as if I were a sheep or a goat. I couldn't slow down. The rock was wet with dew
25   and Lucas's mum's boots were loose without thick socks.

I slipped and then missed my step completely. I remember thinking *This will be bad*, as I was falling and then it all went black.

9 **numb** without feeling – 14 **to shiver** to shake slightly because it is cold – 22 **gap** space, hole – 24 **dew** *Tau*

LUCAS

I was just getting all my books into my backpack when the police car pulled up outside.

Dad was finishing his toast. Mum was mopping up some spilled tea. Lara was in the bathroom – of course.

5　I recognised Sergeant Robinson from a school visit when he'd come in to talk to us about drugs and drug gangs. I opened the door and he said, 'Hello, Lucas. Can I have a word?' and I said yes and felt completely sick.

Dad looked up from his breakfast.

10　''Ere! Wasson? What you been doing, boy?'

Sergeant Robinson raised a hand in greeting.

'It's OK, Dave. He's not in any trouble. Need his help, is all.'

'Sit down,' said Mum, pushing all the breakfast stuff out of the way. 'Cup of tea?'

15　'Proper job,' he said. 'Four sugars. I know, sweet tooth, can't help it.'

He patted his stomach which was flat as could be. Dad grunted.

'Don't know where you put it, Mike. It'll catch up to you one day, you see if it don't. Anyway, what's all this about needing my boy's
20　help?'

Sergeant Robinson turned to me. 'It's about your classmate. Zaynab ...' He looked at his notebook. 'Zaynab Egal.'

My heart nearly stopped.

'What about her?' I heard myself say.

25　'Gone missing. Wasn't in her bed this morning. No sign of her. Any ideas? Do you know where she might have gone? When did you last see her?'

I sat down. My head went empty and then filled up again with panic.

15 **proper job** (*Devon dialect, sl*) excellent – 15 **sweet tooth** (*idm*) a strong liking for sweet foods

'Yesterday. On the bus home.'

'Did she seem OK? Was she her normal self?'

I hesitated and he saw me hesitate.

'Well? Anything you can tell us will be helpful.'

5   'She was very upset about Mrs Baldwin.'

'The head teacher? Was Zaynab in trouble?' He was checking his phone as he spoke. 'Got a team out on the moors, with a dog,' he explained. 'Just checking in case they've found anything.'

'Dear God,' said Mum. 'That poor child.'

10 'Go on. You were saying about Mrs Baldwin.'

Dad was listening intently. Mum sat down next to me and put her arm round my shoulders.

'Well, Zaynab and me and some others have started a group fighting climate change. Mrs Baldwin doesn't like it.'

15 'I knew it!' said Dad. 'You had to get mixed up with that troublemaker foreign kid.'

'Shut up, Dad,' I said. I was nearly crying. 'You don't know anything about her.'

'Go on,' urged Sergeant Robinson. 'Mrs Baldwin ...?'

20 'Mrs Baldwin was horrible to her. Zaynab ... and me ... she's blocking us going on the Climate Strike in Exeter and we'd had loads of ideas for things the school could be doing but she just said Zaynab wanted it to be all about her and that she was making up stories about climate disaster and frightening everyone.'

25 'And Zaynab was upset?'

'Yes, upset and angry. Mrs Baldwin has really been picking on her, saying she's a troublemaker and stuff like that.'

'OK,' Sergeant Robinson said. 'Now, where do you think she would have gone? If she was upset?'

30 'I don't know. She might have gone up Rippon Tor. I showed her the way.'

'I'll pass that on.'

He phoned someone, told them to concentrate on Rippon and that there was airborne help on the way.

35 No sooner had he rung off, than the whirring drone of a helicopter could be heard over the house.

'Well, there's the chopper, now. What about other friends, though? Anyone else she might have gone to?'

'I don't think so. She would've come to me if it was anyone. I think I'm her best friend. No. I *know* I'm her best friend.'

5 Dad practically spat his tea out.

Mum hugged me closer. 'They're doing a good thing, David. I'm proud of Lucas. You should be, too.'

Dad shook his head. 'I don't want to know. I'm off. See ya, Mike.' He picked up his van keys and a flask of tea.

10 Sergeant Robinson nodded and then returned to me.

'Want to come with me to look for her?' he asked.

Mum jumped up, looking terrified. 'But what if ...? I don't want him seeing anything ... anything distressing.'

'Lucas needs to toughen up, Megan,' said Dad, as he put his coat
15 on. 'He's turning into a right mummy's boy. Take him up there, Mike.'

Mum made a small sound like a smothered scream.

'I'd like to go, I'll be fine.'

'I'll drop him at school, Megan,' Sergeant Robinson told Mum, as
20 he stood up. 'Come on, boy. Let's see if we can find her.'

It was a fine day, but very, very cold. If Zaynab had been out all night, she'd have hypothermia, for sure. I had visions of her, face down in water or drowned in a bog. People had died on the moors doing Ten Tors and army exercises. Not often, it was true, but it had
25 happened and Zaynab wasn't exactly used to the moors or to our weather.

'At least it wasn't raining,' Sergeant Robinson said, as if he could read my mind. 'Wasn't windy, neither. I expect she's holed up somewhere, safe and sound. She sounds like a good kid. Sensible.'
30 I sat in the back. I think one of our neighbours saw me go. Great! She'd be telling everyone I'd been picked up by the police.

---

1 **chopper** *(inf)* helicopter – 17 **to smother** ['smʌθə] to prevent from happening –
22 **hypothermia** [ˌhaɪpəθɜːmiə] when the body temperature has become dangerously
low – 23 **bog** an area of land which is very wet and muddy – 24 **Ten Tors** an annual
weekend hike in the southwest of England (**tor** rock formation) – 29 **sensible** wise,
intelligent

Sergeant Robinson was watching me via his mirror. 'So, you're a climate warrior, are you? Tell me about it.'

I explained that we were really only just starting and told him about Fridays for Future, the Climate Strike and the ideas for Mrs
5 Baldwin. I was just getting to the end when we arrived at the layby near Rippon Tor, where an ambulance and two police cars were parked.

'Got a call from a member of the public about your demo,' Sergeant Robinson remarked as he reversed onto the grass. 'I told
10 him he was wasting police time. I suspect said individual wastes quite a lot of things, one way or another.'

He winked at me and I felt my worries vanish for a moment. He was on our side.

'Come on, let's see what's happening. There's PC Popham and
15 Toby.'

It turned out that Toby was a dog. He looked like a German shepherd but with funny ears. He was pulling hard and panting.

'A'right, Constable?' asked Mike, stopping to give Toby a pat.

'Nothing up Rippon Tor, chopper's been over and taken a close
20 look,' said PC Popham, gloomily. 'And Toby here reckons we're on the wrong side of the road. Didn't like it when I crossed. Didn't like it at all.'

'She might have gone to Haytor, itself,' I said. 'I told her it was great, but no fun with tourists there ... but there are no tourists now.'
25 'Too bloody right, there aren't,' snorted PC Popham. 'It's bloody freezing.'

I think I may have turned very pale because he patted me on the shoulder and said, 'She'll be OK, don't you worry. Come on, Tobes, do your stuff.'
30 The dog was straining at his leash.

'Best let him go free, Constable,' said Sergeant Robinson. 'No tourists or dogwalkers to get the wrong idea. Sheep are all down Hound Tor way, seen 'em as I come in from Manaton.'

---

5 **layby** short strip of road by the side where cars can stop for a while – 12 **to vanish** to go away, to disappear – 17 **to pant** to breathe heavily and quickly – 20 **PC** *abbr of* police constable

'Tobes'd never touch a sheep,' the Constable said, irritably. 'Would 'e, boy?'

He let him off the leash and the dog shot off towards Saddle and Haytor.

5 'Blimey, he's in a hurry.'

I was beginning to be very glad that someone was. The longer Zaynab was in the cold, the worse it would be for her.

The ambulance driver wound down his window, he was eating a huge sandwich and spoke with his mouth full. 'We'll just wait here 10 for instructions. You phoned the parents again? Kid might be back home by now.'

Sergeant Robinson shook his head. 'They're under strict orders to call us. They haven't. She's still out there somewhere. Come on, Lucas, let's watch the dog. Reckon he knows.'

15 The helicopter swung high over our heads and towards Saddle Tor.

We watched and waited. It was nearly ten o'clock. I wanted to go and look myself, but Sergeant Robinson said the job was best left to Toby and the chopper, which was zigzagging across the sky, quite 20 low.

'You don't want to be off in the opposite direction when they find her,' he said, kindly. I was glad that he said 'when', not 'if'.

Toby and PC Popham were about a quarter of a mile from us, on the lower slopes of Saddle Tor, amongst the clumps of gorse and 25 bracken. Suddenly, Toby started barking like crazy and PC Popham began waving his arms about like a lunatic.

'Got 'er! And looks like old Tobes was first on the scene. Champion! Let's hope she's OK,' said Sergeant Robinson.

He tapped on the ambulance driver's window. 'Stretcher, please! 30 We've got her.'

A wave of relief washed over me and then the fear returned. What if she was dead?

---

1 **irritably** annoyed, cross – 24 **gorse** *Ginster* – 25 **bracken** *Farn* – 26 **lunatic** madman – 29 **stretcher** long piece of canvas to carry an injured or sick person

ZAYNAB

A dog was standing over me, licking my face.

I love dogs, but I don't like being slobbered all over with their wet tongues and smelling their doggy breath.

I tried to push the dog away, but I could not seem to move.

5   Maybe it was a dream.

I could feel myself drifting off again.

The Red Rebel Brigade stood all around me, staring down at me, silent as ever.

LUCAS

As we got closer, I could see Toby wagging his tail and licking
something on the ground – a little heap of dark clothing. I recognised
Zaynab's bright yellow scarf and coat. I thought I was going to be
sick.

5   PC Popham was trying to get Toby's leash back on, but the dog
seemed to be so pleased to have found her that he really wasn't
being very obedient, especially for a police dog.

'A'right, a'right, Tobes.' PC Popham pulled him away. 'Give the
poor kid some air.'

10 Zaynab was lying on her front, her head twisted to one side and
her leg sticking out at a strange angle. There was blood on her head,
where it had hit a stone.

'Is she …?' I couldn't say the word. She looked so broken, like a
doll. I felt sick with fear.

15 'Am I dead?' Zaynab's voice was very faint.

'*NO!*' we all said at once and I swear Toby said it, too, in his doggy
way. I don't think I have ever felt my heart stop and start again with
such a jolt. I nearly threw up with the relief of it all.

The ambulance crew came running up and shooed us out of the
20 way.

'Broken?' said one, looking at the leg.

'I'd say so, Sherlock,' said the other, drily. 'Get a blanket on her.
I'll ring the hospital. Reckon this is a job for orthopaedics. We'll just
do the vitals and get her on the wagon.'

25 'Lucas?' Zaynab sounded weak and anxious. 'Has my leg come
off?'

I burst out laughing. 'Off? Course not, it's just a bit broken, I think.'

'Feels like it's come off,' she said, sleepily.

---

7 **obedient** doing what you are told – 11 **angle** *Winkel* – 14 **doll** a child's toy which looks
like a small person or baby – 22 **blanket** *Decke* – 24 **vitals** *(pl)* the organs that are
necessary to maintain life

'Hey, Zaynab! I need you to stay awake, my lovely,' said the ambulance driver. 'Lucas, that your name? Can you sit here and talk to her, please? Stop her going to sleep again? We want to keep her awake and alert while we run some checks.'

5   I sat down by her head and stroked her hand.

'What were you doing out on the moors on your own?' I asked.

'You go on your own,' she murmured, closing her eyes.

'Look at me,' I said, quite sharply.

She opened one dark eye.

10 'I don't go out on my own in the middle of the night,' I said, firmly.

'You nearly got run over in the dark,' she replied, a small smile on her lips.

'Yeah. Well, I didn't, did I?'

'I saved you. Now you've saved me. Twice.' She looked pleased.

15 Her eyelids drooped again.

'Zaynab, you have to stay awake. Tell me what happened,' I urged her.

'My head hurts. The Red Rebels came to my room and I went out to find them under the stars.'

20 'Blimey,' said Sergeant Robinson. 'She's proper confused, isn't she? Red Rebels?'

'She'll be saying she was abducted by aliens next,' joked the paramedic.

'Mrs Baldwin spoiled everything,' Zaynab muttered. 'But I'm going
25 to show her. I'll show her ...'

Her voice tailed off.

The ambulance driver, who was obviously the more senior paramedic, looked very serious. 'Right, young lady. We've got to get you on this stretcher. Mike, phone the parents, will you? Need
30 permission to give her a shot before we move her or it'll hurt. A lot.'

'Already done. On their way, meeting us at the ambulance.' Sergeant Robinson looked pleased with himself. 'All's well that ends well, eh?'

---

20 **blimey** *(inf)* used to express surprise, excitement – 23 **paramedic** a person trained to do medical work in case of an emergency *(Rettungssanitäter(in))* – 32 **all's well that ends well** *(idm) Ende gut, alles gut*

'Lucas. I'm Si.' The driver held out his hand and I shook it. 'I need you to keep talking to her, right? You're doing a great job. Zaynab? I'm just going to give you something for the pain and then we are going to have to get you on this stretcher.'

5 He gently pulled up her coat sleeve and stuck a needle in her arm, then he got some large red blocks of foam out of his bag and a bright yellow object that looked a bit like a sleeve with black straps.

'Can you do anything about her leg? Straighten it out?' I asked.

The paramedic looked at me, grimly. 'Oh yes,' he said. 'The fun
10 bit, by which I mean no fun at all. You keep her talking. We'll sort the leg. Got to do it here in case the blood supply is interrupted. She don't want to lose it.'

I couldn't watch and I wished I could have blocked my ears. There was a horrible crunching sound and Zaynab let out a terrifying
15 scream that echoed off the rocks.

'That'll be the shock more than the pain. She's got a fair bit of jollop, in there,' said the other paramedic, Martin, as he strapped on the yellow splint.

Very, very carefully, the paramedics rolled her onto her back and
20 put the blocks either side of her head.

'Neck feels fine, just a precaution. Martin will clean up that gash when we are on board.'

In the distance, I could hear people shouting.

Liban and Deborah were running towards us, stumbling over the
25 tussocks.

'Steady on!' warned PC Popham. 'We've had enough accidents.'

Liban's face was ashen with worry.

'My little girl, my treasure, my princess!' he cried, tears streaming down his face as he bent to kiss her.

30 'Can I come in the ambulance?' he asked.

'Lucas.' Zaynab's voice was weak but insistent. 'Lucas comes with me. Lucas. Only Lucas.'

17 **jollop** *(sl)* pain medication – 18 **splint** long, firm object that is fastened to a broken leg to keep it still – 21 **precaution** an action to prevent sth unpleasant from happening – 21 **gash** long cut, wound – 27 **ashen** very pale

'Best not to distress her, too much, sir. Might as well let the lad go with her,' said Martin.

'I can run you up there in the car, Professor,' said Sergeant Robinson. 'That's no problem.'

Liban agreed, but I knew he wasn't happy.

He gave us a rather sorrowful wave as Martin and Si clipped the stretcher into place and shut the rear doors.

I had never been in an ambulance before. It was a good thing Zaynab had those blocks round her head because it was a really rough ride and the stretcher was made of hard plastic.

'No featherbed for you, Princess,' joked Martin. 'Sorry!'

Zaynab held my hand all the way to the hospital.

'I think I only dreamed about the Red Rebel Brigade,' she said, her eyes half closed. 'I don't think they were there. But a dog was. And you are.'

I squeezed her hand. 'Yes. I'm here and guess what, we're missing school again. It'll do Mrs B's head in!'

She smiled and closed her eyes.

'Oh good. That's a bonus!'

6 **sorrowful** very sad – 10 **rough** uneven, not smooth – 17 **to do sb's head in** *(idm, inf)* to make sb angry

LUCAS

I was like the most popular boy in school for two days. Everyone wanted to know what had happened. There was a story going round that Zaynab had planned to throw herself off the rocks because Mrs Baldwin had been horrible to her.

5 In assembly on the day after Zaynab's accident, an amazing thing happened.

Mr Reeves stood up at the end of assembly and said: 'Today we are initiating the first of many ideas from our Fridays for Future group – daily climate news. Today's news: 11,000 scientists have

10 declared, clearly and unequivocally, that planet Earth is facing a climate emergency and that to secure a sustainable future, we must change how we live. There is no time to lose, the scientists say. The climate crisis has arrived and is accelerating faster than most scientists expected. It is more severe than anticipated, threatening

15 natural ecosystems and the fate of humanity.'

And then he sat down. Mrs Baldwin looked as if she would explode, but I was over the moon! Mr Reeves had actually taken one of our ideas and run with it! Thank goodness we had given him the list, too.

20 Then Aoife stood up.

'What do we want?'

'Climate justice!' shouted Rudy and Jack.

'And when do we want it?'

'Now!' the rest of our group joined in.

25 'What do we want?' Aoife repeated.

'Climate justice!' Most of the school and some of the staff joined in now.

'When do we want it?' Aoife yelled, as Mrs Baldwin shouted at her to stop.

---

10 **unequivocal** definite, certain, leaving no doubt – 14 **to anticipate** to expect, to forecast – 15 **fate** destiny – 17 **over the moon** *(inf)* very pleased about sth

'NOW!' roared the whole school. 'NOW! *NOW!*'

Mrs Baldwin swept out of the hall, her face as black as thunder. The rest of the staff looked amazed or happy or confused or all three.

Mr Reeves stood up again and asked for silence.

5   'It's really great that you feel so passionate about this. Let's make sure we use our passion in the best way possible, eh?'

'What are you going to do, sir?' shouted Rudy.

'What are we all going to do?' added Izzy.

'We are going to be the change,' he said, calmly. 'All of us. But for
10 now, back to your classes. We need to do this properly.'

As we filed out, the noise of people chattering excitedly was almost deafening. It was like a moving wall of sound.

The whole school felt as if it was buzzing. It was amazing. I couldn't wait to tell Zaynab. She would be so proud.

15 There was no assembly the next day but at lunchtime, a Year Ten I didn't know stood on a chair and read out an article from the BBC website, saying that political parties would have to have policies for climate change if they wanted to win over the young.

Everyone in the dining room cheered.

20 Even the dinner ladies banged the lids of the food trays.

I wished Zaynab could have seen all of this.

When school ended and we went outside, Mrs Harris and some other parents were standing there with a huge banner: *Listen to the kids. It's their future.*

25 She beckoned me over.

'We're going to get you all to that Climate Strike event. You tell Zaynab to hurry up and get back here. She's started something and there's no stopping it now.'

When I got home, Mum was already back. She gave me a huge
30 hug and handed over the permission request.

---

12 **deafening** very loud – 20 **lid** the cover of a container

'I got Cath from Rafikis to give me one,' she said. 'I thought you might not dare ask me to fill it in because of your dad. I'm so proud of you, Lucas. You and Zaynab are really making a difference.'

It felt really great to have Mum's support. Would there ever be a time when Dad was proud of me, too? Seeing as he kept on teasing me about going veggie and still snarled at the 'nonsense' of recycling, that time might be a very long way off indeed.

6 **to snarl** *here*: to say sth in an angry way

ZAYNAB

Turned out I had concussion and had fractured my left tibia, really badly. They'd had to put some wire and two pins in to keep the bone stable. I had a kind of metal cage on my leg to make sure the bone ends joined up properly.

5   When I had stopped throwing up from the anaesthetic, I slept for what seemed like days. I had weird dreams, but nothing I could remember. The Red Rebel Brigade didn't pay me another visit.

   The nurses said Father had been in once but that I'd been asleep and he had sat by my bed for a while before giving up and going
10 home. He'd told them that hospitals made him feel very anxious because of Mama and that they could understand with her death being so recent and all that. They said he phoned them three times a day to see how I was. They said he seemed a very lovely dad. So proud of his little girl.

15   When my father wanted to, he could charm the birds out of the trees. That's what Mama used to say.

   'I was a bird in a tree,' she said. 'And he charmed me straight out of it and into his nest.'

   'And then he moved the nest,' I had said, as one of us always said,
20 only back then we laughed happily at Father's power.

   'Yes. He moved the nest and I liked its new location. It felt like home. It *is* home.'

   He moved the nest. Everyone knew that was a bad thing to do, didn't they?

25   No one asked if I was OK about being reminded about my mama.

   I thought about her a lot in between being asleep. I thought about how much time she had had to spend in hospital all on her own, not even in her adopted nest. Now I was just like her. Lying in a

---

1 **concussion** [kənˈkʌʃən] brain injury *(Gehirnerschütterung)* – 1 **tibia** *Schienbein* –
2 **pin** nail – 3 **cage** *Käfig* – 5 **anaesthetic** narcotic, painkiller – 12 **recent** not long ago –
15 **charm the birds out of the trees** *(idm)* to behave in a very charming way

hospital in a foreign country, far away from home. Except I wasn't dying.

She had never complained. She had just tried to keep everything as normal as it could be. She never made me feel bad about not 5 visiting much, she was always so happy to see me. We cried with happiness at being together.

As I lay there on my own, I wished she had asked me to be with her more while she was in hospital. I could have skipped school. It would not have mattered. I wished she was with me right now.

10 I closed my eyes.

Time went by so slowly. Lucas sent me a couple of messages. He promised to come in at the weekend and said that he had some amazing news. I asked him to tell me straight away, but he said he couldn't explain in a message and I'd just have to wait. It felt like 15 that was all I was doing, apart from the routine of performing my prayers as best I could, eating the mush they fed me and staring at the ceiling, sleeping, waiting.

On the third or fourth day, while my favourite nurse, Nurse Baxter, was changing my dressings, she asked me what I was interested in, 20 so I told her.

'You want to listen to a podcast!' she said. 'I love them! I'm not very interested in climate change. It's a bit too stressy for me and I have enough stress here. I listen to podcasts on gardening and cooking. It's amazing what you can learn. Have a look on your phone. 25 We can hook you up to the Wi-Fi.'

The day went much faster with *The Mothers of Invention* and *Costing the Earth*. I listened to people's stories and ideas, and to a thirteen-year-old in America talking about camping outside the UN in a sleeping bag and getting frostbite.

30 Later, when Nurse Baxter came back to check on me before ending her shift, she asked me to tell her about home, so I did. I told her about the families who were camping outside the big cities because they could no longer live off the land after the droughts. I told her

29 **frostbite** *Frostbeule*

106

how the droughts came year after year now, instead of every ten or fifteen years and that they had ruined the lives of the nomads so that they had no hope. When I had finished, she patted my hand and told me that there was nothing like hearing about things in the
5 news from real people.

'You make it matter to me because I can see what it means to you. We've got strange things happening here, too. My sister lives in Yorkshire, she's been flooded out twice now. They can't move because they can't sell their house and my niece gets terrified every
10 time it rains, poor mite, she's only nine. It's you young people who'll have to deal with all this. It's not right.'

When Father came in to visit me in the evening, he looked anxious and distracted.

'Allah be praised! It's good to see you looking better,' he said,
15 pulling up a chair. 'They're going to get you out of bed tomorrow and using crutches. You can come home on Monday, if it all goes well.'

I closed my eyes.

'We need to talk, Zaynab. I can't go on with this constant hostility,'
20 Father said, quietly but insistently. He tried to hold my hand but I wriggled free.

'*I* can,' I said.

'I feel like I've lost you, with this wall of silence you've built around you.'

25 I kept my eyes closed.

'I wanted to talk to you about school. You never told me about the protest you organised. I had to hear it from Bea, the cab driver. And she told me you were in with a rather bad lot ... a girl called Aoife?'

30 'She's not a "bad lot",' I muttered, crossly. 'People misjudge her, make assumptions.'

---

8 **Yorkshire** county in northern England – 10 **mite** *here: (inf)* little child – 13 **distracted** not able to concentrate – 19 **hostility** unfriendly or aggressive behaviour – 30 **to misjudge** to be wrong about sth – 31 **assumption** belief

'Nevertheless, you should have told me what you were up to,' he went on. 'I could have helped.'

'Helped? You live in a bubble, Father. A bubble that only has room for you in it,' I said.

5   I could tell I had hurt him.

'We only have each other, Zaynab,' he replied, after a moment. 'It's you and me against the world, isn't it?'

I shook my head.

'No, Father. It's you and *you*. Always has been.'

10   He looked at me as if I had hit him. He stared at me for what felt like ages. Then he put his head in his hands and said, very softly so I could barely make out the words, 'What would your mama say if she could see us now?'

I buried my face in my pillow and kept it there while he stroked
15   my hair. He must have thought I was crying. What he did not know was that my fists were clenched and I was silently screaming. Now he mentioned her and used her as a weapon to give me pain.

At long last, he left and I was glad he had gone.

10 **to feel like ages** *(idm)* to feel like forever – 17 **weapon** *Waffe*

LUCAS

We couldn't believe it! Mrs Baldwin stood up in assembly and said she was pleased to announce that, after consultation with the governors, a group of parents had got together and paid for a coach to take fifty-five pupils to attend the Climate Strike. She didn't *look*
5 that pleased, but who cared? We were going ... or some of us were, anyway.

Aoife whooped and punched the air as clapping and cheering burst out.

Mrs Baldwin bellowed above the noise: 'Thank you, that is quite
10 enough. Before you go, I have been asked to update you on Zaynab Egal from Year Eight, after her little escapade on the moors. She'll be on crutches and back in school on Tuesday.'

Well, the whole place erupted. Some people even started chanting 'Zaynab! Zaynab! Zaynab!'
15 Mrs Baldwin left the hall and Mr Reeves took over, letting the hubbub die down.

'Everyone is just a bit hyper, I know,' he observed, drily. 'Let's just calm down, focus and pull together to see what we can achieve as a school. OK?'
20 'OK!' we shouted.

Not a single bit of new information got stored in my brain that day because my mind was in a whirl.

Everyone was very excited on the bus home, but I didn't really listen. I felt exhausted and when I got back, I just went to my room
25 and crashed out on the bed, too tired to even work on the banner.

Mum came up later with a mug of hot chocolate.

---

2 **consultation** discussion – 3 **coach** bus – 11 **escapade** [ˌeskəˈpeɪd] dangerous adventure – 16 **hubbub** noise made by a lot of people all talking and shouting at the same time – 22 **in a whirl** *(idm)* very excited and unable to think clearly – 26 **mug** cup

'I'd really love to hear about what you and Zaynab have been doing,' she said. 'When you feel like it. I am not sure what your dad makes of it all, though. Probably best not to talk when he's around.'

'I don't really mind what he thinks,' I said, sipping on the
5 chocolate. 'It won't stop me doing what I'm doing.'

'Well, you never know,' she said. 'He might surprise you.'

I don't think either of us thought that was ever really going to happen.

'You're growing up, beginning to make your own way in the world.
10 I'm proud of you,' she said, and there was a tinge of sadness in her voice. 'But you'll always be my precious baby. You know that, don't you?'

I managed to suppress a cringe. We hugged and she went downstairs.

15 I fell asleep and missed tea.

Dad knocked on my door around nine-thirty and handed me a plate with a fat cheese sandwich on it – one of his doorstep specials.

'Your mother says you've had quite a week, one way and another,' he said, gruffly, as he turned to go out. 'Is that kid OK?'

20 'I'm going to visit her in hospital tomorrow,' I said.

'Bloody daft going up on the moors in the middle of the night. Lucky for her they found her,' he said and shut the door.

I ate the sandwich gratefully and then crashed out again.

The next day I did most of my chores as quickly as I could, and then
25 caught the bus to the hospital. I'd drawn a quick 'get well' card which showed Zaynab galloping across the moors on the back of a giant version of Toby, the rescue dog, and Mum had given me some flowers that had gone past their sell-by date. They looked a bit minging to be honest, but I couldn't refuse to take them without
30 hurting her feelings. I did think I might just stuff them in a bin, but then I decided it would be really nice for Zaynab to know that my mum had been thinking about her.

10 **tinge** a small amount – 13 **to suppress** to hide, to block – 21 **daft** *(inf)* stupid –
29 **minging** *(inf)* disgusting, ugly

'Flowers for your girlfriend?' a porter teased me in the lift.

'Guess so,' I said, and I could feel myself turn scarlet. I hoped I would be back to normal by the time I reached the ward.

She was in a room on her own. She had earphones in and was listening intently, eyes shut. I crept up and said, 'Boo!'

'Hey, there, Ghost Boy! At last!' She was so pleased to see me, she grinned from ear to ear.

'Wow!' I said. 'Are those *staples* in your head?'

She had a row of little metal strips across her forehead.

'Yes. Do you like them? I am going for the Frankenstein look. Check out my leg!'

'You mean Frankenstein's monster,' I corrected her, as she flipped aside the blanket to show me. 'Ugh! That is so gross!' I pretended to be sick.

Actually, it really was quite gross. She had two metal rods down either side of her leg and bolts sticking into bloody holes in the flesh.

'I know!' she said, thrilled with the effect. 'It's disgusting, isn't it? Hey! Are those for me?'

I was still clutching the nearly-dead flowers.

'Yeah. Sorry. They're from Mum. Sorry about them being a bit ...' I tailed off.

'They'll last the two days!' she said. 'And that's enough. I'll be out of here! Sit down. Tell me everything.'

I pulled up the chair to her bedside and then remembered my card, which had got a bit squashed in my pocket.

'You can open this and then you need to tell me everything, first,' I said.

Zaynab tore open the envelope.

'I love it! You are so good at art, Lucas. You are a real genius. I expect this will be worth a lot of money one day!'

---

1 **porter** sb who helps out with patients in a hospital – 3 **ward** room where patients in a hospital stay – 13 **gross** (*inf*) disgusting, horrible, unpleasant – 16 **bolt** *Schraube* – 18 **thrilled** very happy, delighted

'Yeah, right!' I said, feeling my face going rather hot again. 'But, right now, like I said, I need to know why you were out on the moors. Was it because Mrs B had upset you?'

Zaynab snorted.

5 'Yeah, she'd upset me, but she had nothing to do with me being on the moors. I just had a weird dream. The Red Rebel Brigade were in it and then I woke up and couldn't get back to sleep. I just wanted to feel a bit like I did at home, when we all went out into the desert to spend a night under the stars and I wanted to see the dawn and
10 say my prayers and know that I was seeing the same sun that was already shining in my country. And, yes, I wanted to get away from everything ... but not, you know, get away from *everything*.'

She put out her hand and I held it for a moment, feeling embarrassed and relieved at the same time.

15 'And then you came and rescued me. Again. Jazakallah.'

I shook my head. 'Don't thank me. It was Toby, the dog. He found you. I sent them all the wrong way, up Rippon Tor.'

Zaynab laughed. 'I'm only here for six months. I am not going to go up the same tor twice, am I?'

20 Six months. I had forgotten about that. When the spring came, she would be gone.

Zaynab reached for my hand again. Seemed like she could read my mind. 'No time for being sad about that, now,' she said, seriously. 'We've got stuff to do! Now. Tell me!'

25 So, I told her about the daily climate news, the parents' plan for getting us to the Climate Strike and how Mrs Baldwin had agreed to let some of us go.

'Wow! Who got to her, do you think?' she asked, eyes shining with excitement.

30 'I don't know. Maybe she just felt bad because of what happened to you?'

'Nah, she's not like that. She will have worked out that it's good publicity for the school. She's just like the people Father works with.'

9 **dawn** time of the day when the light first appears

'Everyone is waiting for you to come back to school,' I went on. 'You're going to get the most massive welcome.'

'I guess I am getting a bit of a sympathy vote, huh?' she asked, picking at a hole in the blanket.

5 I disagreed. 'It's not sympathy, it's something else, something very different. It's like everyone wants a hero and you are it. Even Mum says you are becoming a celeb. Bet you never thought that would happen when you came to Devon!'

Zaynab looked worried. 'It mustn't be about me,' she said. 'Mrs
10 B said I was making it all about me, that I just wanted to be the centre of attention. That can't happen, or she'll be right.'

'Of course she won't be right!' I said. 'You haven't *tried* to be a hero. We've all decided you are! That's different! You've got practically the whole school behind you!'

15 She didn't look as if she believed me. She began to cry.

'What if it doesn't last? What if people go to the Climate Strike because they get to miss school and then they go back to being bored with it all? It'll soon be just us again, trying to get people to do stuff. And what if we are just shouting in the wind? What if
20 nothing changes?'

'Rubbish!' I said. 'You've changed things forever, you'll see.'

She blew her nose noisily and lay back on her pillows.

A nurse came over to see what was going on. 'You feeling a bit tired, my lovely?' she said cheerily, as she swept up the flowers and
25 the pile of used tissues. 'You have a little cat nap. I'm sure your friend won't mind. I'll have to take these away, I'm afraid. The days of flowers by patients' beds are long gone.'

She turned to me. 'Really takes it out of you, a bad break does. Makes you depressed, people don't realise. Poor kid, she's been very
30 brave but it'll be a while before she gets back to normal.'

Zaynab's eyes were closed but she reached out for my hand again.

'I'm sorry, Lucas. I get so miserable all of a sudden. And tired, so tired. Sorry.'

7 **celeb** *abbr of* celebrity – 25 **cat nap** short sleep

She drifted off to sleep.

I really wanted to tell her about my banner and that I planned to show how what we did here made things worse for people in Zaynab's country, but I guessed that could wait. I made some more doodles of it in my notebook and a small sketch of Zaynab's face.

I sat by her bed, hoping she might wake up, for about twenty minutes and then the nurse came back and said it was time for me to go.

'I'll explain to her that you couldn't stay longer,' she said, kindly. 'You're Lucas, aren't you? I'm Nurse Baxter. She talks a lot about you. It's good she's got such a loyal friend. She's a long way from home, isn't she?'

She walked with me to the lift.

'Just a thought, Lucas. If you come in tomorrow afternoon, you could help her with her crutches. We had a first go today and she didn't find it very easy. I think she'd get on better with you there.'

'I'd love to help, if she'll let me,' I said.

'Oh, she'll let you, I'm sure. She's sometimes not as tough as she makes out, is she?'

'Maybe not, but she's a fighter,' I said.

'Oh yes!' smiled the nurse. 'No doubt about that!'

ZAYNAB

I was really upset when I woke up and found Lucas had gone. He had come all that way to see me and I'd just fallen asleep!

Nurse Baxter told me that he had waited for a while but that she'd had to chuck him out when visiting hours were over.

5 'What a lovely boy!' she said. 'So polite and so caring. And tomorrow, he'll be back. Promised to help with your crutches, he has. Bless him!'

The next day, I got back from hobbling to the bathroom to find Lucas and Father sitting on either side of my bed, deep in conversation.
10 Lucas was telling Father that all he really wanted to do one hundred per cent of the time was to campaign against climate change.

'This is very admirable, Lucas. I applaud you, as I applaud all young people who care about the environment,' Father said, while looking at me as if to say, 'See how well I get on with your friend!'
15 'It's really because of Zaynab. She's the one who inspires us,' Lucas replied, and now *he* was looking over to check if it was OK to talk about me.

'That is good to hear,' Father said.

Lucas went on, 'So, anyway. What are Jurassic Oil and Gas like?
20 To work for, I mean.'

Father's eyebrows shot up and I flashed Lucas a warning look.

Lucas flushed scarlet. 'Zaynab told me a bit about your work. I think it's really good if companies want to try and put things right; so long as they do something really useful.'
25 Father looked from Lucas to me and back again. 'I had not realised that Zaynab had taken any interest in my work, which is confidential, by the way. She has a rather low opinion of businesses and their

4 **to chuck sb out** (*inf*) to ask sb to leave − 12 **admirable** praiseworthy, great −
26 **confidential** secret − 27 **business** company

motivation ... and that is understandable, but without them, real change will never happen.'

'I guess so,' Lucas said, almost squirming in his chair while I glared at him. 'I looked them up on the Internet. There was an article on
5 them. It looked interesting ... what they said they were doing. Improving the housing for poor people, planting trees and stuff.'

Father nodded. 'Yes, they have a good programme of investment in climate-affected areas, one which, I hope, will be rolled out in my country, if my work is successful and Allah wills it.'

10 'What do they want in return?' I asked. 'Mama always said these companies don't do good stuff for nothing.'

A look of annoyance passed over Father's face. 'Doing the right thing is good business.'

'And would Mama have liked what they're doing – what you're
15 doing?' I persisted.

'Zaynab, my precious one, you have all your mother's cynicism, with none of her realism. You and Lucas ... what you are doing with so much passion, that is good, it is a fine thing. But in the real world, change must come from beyond your bubble.'

20 *Bubble!* I thought to myself, furiously. *We'll show him who is in a bubble!*

Lucas looked very uncomfortable to be in the middle of this and I couldn't blame him.

'Father, can you go and get me a book or something from the
25 shop?' I asked, in an effort to get him to go.

'I brought you a book, actually!' Lucas was clearly relieved to have a distraction. He pulled out a bright pink paperback. 'Cath from Rafikis café gave it to Mum yesterday so I could give it to you.'

The book was *This Is Not a Drill; An Extinction Rebellion*
30 *Handbook.*

Father shook his head. I knew what he was thinking – people like Mama, stirring things up.

---

3 **to squirm** to move from side to side because you are nervous or embarrassed –
15 **to persist** to continue, to carry on – 16 **cynicism** belief that people always act selfishly

I put it on the bedside table and looked at Lucas as fiercely and meaningfully as I could.

'What?' he asked. That boy was so thick sometimes.

'I think,' said Father, 'that Zaynab would like me to get out of your
5 way for a bit. I understand. I'll go and make some calls.'

'Sorry about that,' Lucas said miserably, once Father had gone. 'I've made trouble, haven't I?'

I shrugged. 'He'll forget about it, he's not that interested in us. Tell me about Jurassic Oil and Gas.'

10 Lucas looked uncomfortable.

'I will, but first, what is going on with you and him? Don't you want him to help us? I really think he could, I think he wants to. He was really listening to me while you were in the bathroom.'

I started leafing through the Extinction Rebellion handbook,
15 refusing to look up.

'Fine, go ahead, ask him. All he wants is for you to like him, then he can feel good and then he'll let you down, just when you need him.'

Lucas fell silent and it began to annoy me. We were wasting time.
20 'OK. You want to know what he has done to make me not trust him? He has wiped Mama from his life, from our lives, as if she were never there. He never talks about her work, her achievements. There are families who depended on her. Did Father step in to help? No! He doesn't even rate what she did. And he doesn't care that *I* need
25 her, that I'm on my own without her. But, sure, cosy up to him. Maybe you'll get somewhere because you're a boy.'

Tears were pouring down my face. Lucas squeezed my hand. I snatched it away and turned my face into my pillow. 'I miss my mama. I miss her *so* much!'

30 Then Father came back. I quickly wiped my eyes and pretended to be too tired to talk anymore and asked them both to go.

---

2 **meaningfully** in a way that is meant to express a feeling or thought without saying it – 3 **thick** *here:* stupid – 22 **achievement** act of having succeeded – 24 **to rate** to decide whether sth is good or bad – 25 **to cosy up** to seek to become close to sb

'Message me!' Lucas mouthed as he followed my father out. '*Please*.'

Nurse Baxter wasn't happy when she came with the crutches for my practice. 'Where's Lucas gone? We need him.'

5   'Do we?' I said. 'I can manage fine without him.'

Even as I said it, I knew it wasn't true.

LUCAS

'Was she in pain?' Liban asked as we travelled down in the lift. 'Or
was she upset about something else? Perhaps you can help me,
Lucas?'

Zaynab's words were ringing in my ears. *He has wiped Mama*
5 *from our lives.*

'Lucas?' Liban was staring at me. 'Are you OK?'

'Yeah, fine, sorry. I was just thinking.'

'Can I tempt you to a cup of tea, before the bus? Or a Coke, or
whatever you like? I'd really like your advice,' Liban said, smiling
10 and pointing at the hospital café.

'Yeah, sure.' I'd made up my mind to tell him straight.

We sat down in a corner. I had a hot chocolate. Not that nice. A
big lump of instant choc powder suspended in boiling water. I stirred
it hard until it dissolved. I could feel myself putting off the moment
15 when one of us spoke again.

'As I know you are aware,' he began, sipping his mint tea, 'I have
a difficult relationship with Zaynab. Everyone tells me that girls get
difficult at this age and, of course, it does not help that we have lost
her mother.'

20 'Why don't you talk to her?' I blurted out. 'Zaynab says you act
like her mum was never there, like you've erased her or something.'

It was as if I had hit him. He dropped the cup and spilled the tea
all over the table.

'Sorry,' I said, grabbing handfuls of serviettes to mop it up. 'Sorry,
25 I didn't mean to say that.'

'But it *is* what she said, isn't it?' he asked, looking at me intently.

'Yes, just now, before you came back. She thinks you've forgotten
all about her mum, as if she never existed.'

---

8 **to tempt** to try to make sb want sth by making it attractive – 13 **instant** powder to
prepare a drink quickly

Liban covered his face with his hands and was silent for a while. Then he sat up and looked straight at me.

'I miss Fran – Zaynab's mother – more than I can say.' He paused. 'And Zaynab reminds me so much of Fran. Not to look at, no, but
5 her spirit, her determination, her passion ... It's a painful reminder.' He looked away.

'You don't have to tell me anything,' I said. 'It's none of my business. I shouldn't have said anything.'

'Of course you should. I am grateful to you, Lucas, truly I am.'
10 He took out his wallet and handed me a photo. The woman was very beautiful. Zaynab had the same large, fierce eyes, but this woman's were a deep green instead of brown and her hair the fiery red of bracken in the autumn. I handed the photo back and he studied it for a few moments before returning it to his wallet.

15 'Fran was an amazing woman. Very positive, determined. Full of energy. Zaynab is like her, very like her, maybe *too* like her. Fran was stubborn, impulsive. When I met her, she was campaigning for human rights and teaching English to immigrant families in Bristol, especially women, encouraging them to integrate, determined to
20 help them succeed in a strange land. She was always on the side of the underdog.'

He looked away for a moment and seemed to be gathering his thoughts.

'Sorry, this must be very boring for you,' he muttered.
25 I shook my head.

He sighed and went on, '... That's why, when my work took me back home, she decided to come and work with nomads driven off the land by drought. She became increasingly interested in global warming and desertification. She saw how climate change was
30 destroying lives and she was absolutely determined to do something, to make a difference. So she threw herself into volunteering in the camps. Hard work. Dangerous work, but she got satisfaction from

---

9 **grateful** thankful – 10 **wallet** purse – 21 **underdog** person who seems least likely to succeed, loser – 29 **desertification** process by which a piece of land becomes dry, empty and infertile – 32 **satisfaction** joy, pleasure

helping individuals. They loved her as one of their own. She had a passion for people and for changing lives. It is this passion that runs in Zaynab's veins.'

He took a deep breath.

5 'I was wrapped up in my work, she involved Zaynab in hers. We did not always agree on the best way to make change happen, it's true.'

He looked at me again, as if he was checking to see if I was still listening. I was.

10 'Anyway, she became gravely ill without warning. Sometimes it felt as if she wanted to be gone as quickly as possible, so we wouldn't suffer. There was nothing to be done. They could not have cured her here in the UK, either, though maybe Zaynab believes differently. I know she wishes that it was me who had been taken, rather than

15 Fran.'

'I'm sure she doesn't,' I said, trying to reassure him, but feeling that it might be a little bit true.

'You can see how much hostility there is! She's angry with me. And maybe she's right, I've pushed the grief away. I've left her to

20 sort herself out, because I don't know what to say or do and because I cannot give her what she got from her mother – the drive, the inspiration. I know that. I thought it would help to get away from it all. Seems I was wrong.'

He coughed. I think it was to cover up the fact that he was nearly

25 crying.

I patted his back, feeling helpless.

'You have to tell Zaynab,' I said. 'You have to put this right. She can't go on believing that you don't care.'

'But I have been a bad father to her, haven't I? I have left her to

30 grieve on her own, to battle on her own. I have taken her away from her home so that I am not reminded of my loss. How can I be anything but a bad father after that?'

---

10 **gravely** seriously – 19 **grief** feeling of extreme sadness – 21 **drive** energy, determination – 30 **to grieve** to mourn, to be very sad about sth

I shrugged. 'I don't know. You tried to make things better for her. But you've got to talk to Zaynab now, that's all that matters.'

He sniffed noisily and then stood up, reaching over to pat my shoulder.

5 'You are a good friend to her, Lucas. Thank you. I will go and speak with her now. We cannot go on like this, either of us.'

I sat there for a while, feeling sick and overwhelmed. Too much emotion. Too much unhappiness.

ZAYNAB

When Father came back into my room, I knew that Lucas had told him what I had said and, for a moment, I was angry with Lucas. He had no business interfering.

I barely heard what Father said.

5 I had forgotten how to feel anything but angry. I had a sort of rushing sound in my ears.

Some words began to come through, about Mama making Father promise to try to make life normal, as if she had never been there, to move on, live life, not waste time grieving. I didn't know whether
10 to believe him. He'd never mentioned this promise before and nor had she. Was he making it up to make himself feel better about forgetting her?

Then I remembered how Mama had said that the last days we passed together in her room, overlooking the garden, were the best
15 days of her life, but that my best days were still to come. I could see her so clearly, feel the touch of her frail hand in mine, hear her voice. 'You will fly, my darling, I know it. You will fly.'

Now, I could hear myself saying over and over and over, 'You just didn't seem to care. I was so angry. So lonely. You wiped her from
20 our lives, like you wanted to forget her, like you didn't care.'

'I care. I care very much,' he repeated, over and over again. 'I got it wrong, I see that now. I got it wrong ...'

He put his arms round me and I felt myself gradually relax and lean into him. He stroked my hair and made soothing noises.

25 Somewhere, a bit of me was still frozen, like the sliver of ice in Kai's heart in *The Snow Queen,* which Mama used to read to me when I was little. Father and I had been like polite strangers for so long that I'd forgotten what it was like to feel like I was anything to him at all. Now it actually felt good to be held close. I could almost
30 believe that he would never let me go.

24 **soothing** having a calming effect

After a while, we separated and dried our eyes.

'Your mama would be very proud of you, Zaynab,' he said, taking my chin in his hand and looking at me intently. 'You walked in her footsteps and now you make footprints of your own. Let's speak of her from now on. Every day.'

'Do you promise?' I asked him.

'I promise. And you and I, we must share more. I want you to see that we are on the same side, working towards the same goals. I would appreciate your support, just as you supported your mother.'

I hesitated and he saw me hesitate.

'I understand,' he said, patting my hand. 'We must rebuild. Inshallah.'

'Inshallah.'

Could I ever trust him the way I had trusted Mama?

ZAYNAB

I was getting to be pretty good with my crutches by the time the hospital let me out. Nurse Baxter came in to say goodbye, even though it wasn't her shift.

'Go get 'em, girl!' she said. 'And good luck at that demo! You make
5 sure you've got a good placard, mind. I want to see you on my TV!'

It felt strange, going back to Hope Cottage. Father was just a bit too much. Too huggy. Too smiley. Too everything. He seemed to be able to just zero everything as if we'd never had a problem.

'I've been so hoping that you two would sort things out,' Deborah
10 said as she carried my bag into her study. She'd made a bed for me on the little sofa because there was no way I could get up the steep stairs to my room in the eaves.

'We have made a start,' I said, cautiously.

'Toffee has missed you,' she said, as he came into the room and
15 jumped up for a stroke. 'Just be careful that he doesn't trip you up. I hate to think what would happen if you fell on that leg. Ugh. It really is quite gruesome, isn't it?'

I was wearing a pair of trousers she'd found in a charity shop with one leg split open so that I could get them on over the Frankenstein
20 bolts.

Bea the cabbie, as we called her now, had offered to drive me to school the next day, but I said no. Lucas came to help me hobble to the bus stop and on to the bus. He wanted to ask about Father and I wanted to hear more about Jurassic Oil and Gas, but it was
25 impossible. Everyone wanted to come and take a look at my leg and squeal with disgust. I felt like an exhibit in a museum or something. To be honest, it was also a bit of a relief. I didn't know how I felt about what Lucas had done. I realised it meant that I did not totally

---

3 **shift** *Schicht* – 7 **huggy** *(inf)* tending to hug sb a lot – 12 **in the eaves** *here: unter dem Dach* – 21 **cabbie** *(inf)* taxi driver – 26 **exhibit** an object that is shown in a museum

believe in the new, interested and considerate Father. Was it all for show?

There was no time to talk about any of it, anyway. In assembly, Mrs Baldwin announced the names of the pupils who had been
5 selected to go to the big demonstration and, to my surprise, our group had been given priority.

'I know!' said Aoife, catching up with me as I hobbled down the main corridor. 'You gotta ask who put the screws on Mrs B, eh?'

'Just guilt, if you ask me,' said Sophie-Ann. 'She's realised that
10 she's swimming against the tide.'

At lunch, the twins were besides themselves with excitement and chattering about what they were going to wear. They began to irritate me.

'It's not a party,' I snapped. 'We have to have an aim, a purpose,
15 a message. Just like Rudy's mum said.'

I shut my eyes and tried to get back to how I felt at the Fridays for Future demo. I made myself conjure up pictures of people in the displacement camps, living in tents, without enough to eat. I thought about Mama and the team teaching the women and girls
20 how to stay safe, setting them up with some money or equipment, like sewing machines, so they could start small businesses and have some control over their lives. What would they want me to do? What would my country want me to do?

'Are you OK?' Lucas looked worried.

25 'Yes. I'm fine. Just thinking.'

Everyone was watching me closely.

'I think I want to make people understand that things we do here end up really hurting people in poor countries. My country isn't pumping out CO2, but we're the ones paying the price, and not just
30 with droughts and hunger, but kids missing school, girls being scared of being attacked in the camps or being sold. It's much worse for girls than boys. All of it.'

---

1 **considerate** kind – 10 **to swim against the tide** *(idm)* to resist (the general opinion) –
14 **aim** intention, plan – 14 **purpose** reason for which sth is made or done –
17 **to conjure up** to make sth appear – 21 **sewing machine** *Nähmaschine*

'I don't know how anyone can let those children starve and die,' Poppy said, quietly.

I took a deep breath. 'My mama said that the governments of rich countries think we are worth nothing because we have no money to spend on their stuff, so it does not really matter if we die before our lives have even really begun.'

'You'll have to speak at the rally,' Aoife said. 'It's a massive opportunity. There'll be hundreds of people there.'

'They'll never forget you, Zaynab. You do stand out because of what you say and how you say it,' Lucas added.

'Stand out for the right reasons,' Mrs Baldwin had said. Maybe the moment was coming.

LUCAS

On Friday, it was straight off the school bus and straight onto the coach.

The chatter was at fever pitch, but everyone stopped and clapped Zaynab as she hobbled down to the back where Aoife, as usual, had
5   bagged seats. Everyone was wearing green clothes. Aoife had painted her face green and looked super weird. I had been a bit worried about finding anything to wear, but Mum dug out one of Dad's old fishing sweaters from the bottom of their wardrobe. It was a bit skanky, to be honest, but it was definitely green. I'd stuffed it into
10 my backpack with the banner, in case Dad asked any questions.

I felt almost sick with excitement and I think Zaynab felt the same way. A bit further up the bus, Mr Reeves sat holding the megaphone that was used on Sports Day.

'We can borrow that so everyone can hear your speech,' I
15 whispered to Zaynab.

She looked nervous.

'What if I can't do it? What if no one listens?'

'You can and they will!' I reassured her.

She took out her notes.
20 'I keep reading the speech,' she said, 'but it just doesn't seem to stick in my head. It's like it just slides out. I can't practise at all. What if I can't remember what to say? I'll look a real idiot.'

I knew I'd be practically wetting myself if I was about to speak in public, but that was no use to Zaynab.
25 'Just do what you did in the meeting. Just say what is in your head. You know why you're doing this. You just have to tell them,' I said, squeezing her hand. 'And it's not about you, is it? That's what you keep saying. I think it is … a bit. A bit about you and your mama …

---

3 **at fever pitch** extremely excited – 5 **to bag** *(inf)* to take – 9 **skanky** *(inf)* dirty, unattractive – 21 **to slide** *here:* to vanish, to go away – 23 **to wet oneself** to urinate on yourself because you are nervous

but that doesn't matter because what you're going to say is important for everyone to hear.'

All of this occurred to me while I was speaking. Of course it was about her. And me. And all the others. We all had our own reasons. I wanted to be different from my dad. I wanted to make Zaynab proud of me. I wanted to be part of something big and important. But none of that mattered so long as we made people think more about how they could make a change.

The driver dropped us off near the Cathedral. People stopped to look at our placards. They were all really good, but some were absolutely brilliant.

Back to School
When Earth is Cool

Don't be a fossil fool

I LIKE MY CHOCOLATE HOT,
NOT MY PLANET

YOUR MESS
OUR FUTURE

The dinosaurs thought they
had loads of time, too.

Actually, lots of people thought *my* banner was brilliant and asked me if they could take pictures of it. They loved the way I'd painted the car with black smoke pouring out, making a trail all the way to a desert with a cow skeleton, the thin little girl with huge eyes and the words *Stop Burning Sunlight!* spelled out in flames.

We walked towards the big shopping centre. We'd been practising the chants which Rudy's mum had found on the Internet and now we were absolutely belting them out so that our voices bounced off the walls of the shops.

5 *'Hey! Hey! Ho! Ho!*
Climate change has got to go!'
and
'Climate change is not a lie
Do not let our planet die!'

10 People stood aside to let us through. Some clapped us. A few shouted insults.

'Did you hear what those people said?' Poppy was shocked when a couple told her she was a 'something' idiot child who should be in school. 'So rude! So horrid!'

15 Zaynab smiled. 'They are frightened of us, that's good!'

'Yeah!' said Aoife, punching the air. 'Kid power is coming!'

We turned the corner to enter the shopping square. I think nearly all of us squealed or said 'wow' or screamed.

So many people! Hundreds. More arriving from every direction.

20 Banners, placards, flags. It was beautiful. Really, really beautiful.

I glanced at Zaynab and she looked as if she was on fire.

'We are going to do this,' she said, in a low voice full of determination. 'No one can stop us now.'

A new school group joined from the far end. They had drums and

25 they beat out a wild rhythm.

Aoife groaned. 'How could I forget my bodhrán?' she wailed.

The drums beat louder and louder. The chanting followed their beat. It felt like we were all part of one creature, one being. We felt excited, happy.

30 Suddenly, a placard in the distance caught my eye, I pointed it out to Zaynab.

'Look ... *Jurassic Oil and Gas wants our extinction.'*

'We need to speak to that person,' Zaynab said. 'Let's try to get closer.'

---

3 **to belt out** *(inf)* to sing very loudly

I know how much Zaynab hated her crutches, but they are super useful when you want to get through a crowd! Most people's attention was on an older boy up at the front, standing on a sort of platform, holding a microphone, but even so, they took a moment
5 to smile at us and say nice things about my banner.

The boy was getting the crowd to make some noise.

'What do we want?' he shouted.

'Climate justice!' the crowd replied.

'When do we want it?'

10 'NOW!'

The roar was deafening.

'My name is Justin and I am a student at the University,' he said. 'I am studying Renewable Energy.'

We heard Aoife's unmistakable voice shout out, 'No more coal,
15 no more oil, keep that carbon in the soil!'

Everyone cheered.

'Yes! Exactly! Thank you!' Justin said.

Justin gave a short speech about why he was out on the streets. Then he invited up the local MP, Francis Fanshawe, to speak. The
20 crowd booed.

'Hey! Stop! Not all politicians are bad,' Justin said, 'and here we are really lucky to have a climate champion who cycles everywhere!'

Everyone cheered and whooped.

We sort of half-listened to him thanking us as we got closer to the
25 young man with the placard. He was listening intently, but Zaynab got his attention.

'Jurassic Oil and Gas. What do you know about them?' she asked, urgently.

The guy looked a bit annoyed. 'They're scammers, greenwashers.
30 Why?'

'We know someone who is working with them,' Zaynab said. 'We are a bit suspicious.'

---

29 **scammer** *(inf)* swindler *(Betrüger(in))* – 29 **greenwasher** a company that pretends to be more environmentally friendly than it really is – 32 **suspicious** [sə'spɪʃəs] not trusting sth or sb

'You're right to be,' he replied. 'I'm an environmental activist and I've been tracking these scammers for over a year, but I can't talk now, I need to hear the speeches for my blog. Give me your number, I'll call you. I'm Max. Nice banner, by the way.'

5 He took a photo of the banner and then he and Zaynab swapped numbers.

We focused our attention back on the stage.

'You young people, you are our hope. Never, ever stop telling truth to power!' Mr Fanshawe punched the air and the drums started
10 up again. Some people started dancing and chanting.

Suddenly, I saw Liban, standing above the crowd on one of the metal benches, scanning the crowd for Zaynab. He saw us and waved and started making his way slowly through the tightly packed crowd. Then his face changed as he read the placard behind us.

15 'Did you know he was coming?' I asked. 'He looks pretty unhappy.'

'Yes, he texted. You know what? I do not care if he's unhappy,' Zaynab said. 'He shouldn't be working with an oil company. Let's move.'

Just then, a woman from Extinction Rebellion took over the
20 microphone and invited anyone who wanted to speak to come to the stage.

'Go on, Zaynab!' I urged. 'This is your chance!'

She gave me a look of pure panic, which quickly changed into defiance.

25 'You are right, it is!' she said. People got out of the way again as she hobbled through the crowd and up onto the wooden box that served as a stage.

I think we were all holding our breath as she took the microphone.

'My name is Zaynab and I am from a country that doesn't exist
30 because of politics and may soon be no more than a desert because of climate change.'

Everyone was silent. She had them in her power. I thought my heart would burst. She was my friend. My best friend.

---

22 **to urge** to encourage strongly – 24 **defiance** resistance, opposition

'Preserve the earth for it is your mother. These are the instructions of the Holy Prophet, peace be upon Him. We love our mother, don't we?' Zaynab began. 'She has looked after and put up with us humans mining, drilling, consuming and destroying for long enough. Now it is time to look after her or she will die and we will die with her. Let me tell you what you can do to make a difference to children just like us, back in my country ...'

Only I knew what these words really meant to Zaynab and where they were coming from. I looked round for Liban. He had nearly got to where I was standing. His expression was a mixture of pride and something else. Irritation? Sadness?

---

1 **to preserve** to make sure sth stays as it is, to maintain – 4 **mining** industry that gets minerals, coal etc. out of the ground – 4 **drilling** process of cutting holes in the surface of the earth to get oil

ZAYNAB

Someone helped me up on to the stage, which was not easy with my leg.

I took the microphone. Just as I feared, my speech had vanished from my head. I had no idea what I was going to say.

5 'Keep the mic close to your lips,' the XR woman whispered. 'Good luck!'

I closed my eyes for a second or two and cleared my throat.

And then it just came out. The earth as our mother, whom we loved, dying if we didn't save her. Mama was in my heart and in my
10 mind as I spoke. I almost didn't know what I was saying, but I could see that people were listening and the words just kept coming.

'There's a charity, CrisisAid, it looks after the victims of war, famine and climate change. And, you know what? When the desert keeps growing because of global warming and safe, family homes keep
15 vanishing and emergency camps keep growing, guess who suffers the most? Girls and women. They are the poorest. They are the most vulnerable. They aren't thought worth educating. They have babies before they are ready. They struggle to feed their children. They walk miles for food and water. They can be sold, exploited, raped.

20 'I am a girl, like them, but I am lucky. I am privileged, I know, and I am trying to earn that privilege. My mama worked for CrisisAid until she was too ill to carry on and sometimes I was lucky enough to be with her. It's an amazing thing to change a life, to see kids being able to smile, laugh, play, go to school, eat and sleep safely
25 every day. Kids like little Halima, only six, she walked seventy kilometres for a bowl of food. I was ten when I met her. I could pick her up as if she were a doll, a doll with twigs for legs.'

---

12 **famine** ['fæmɪn] situation in which many people have no or little food –
17 **vulnerable** to be weak and easy to hurt – 19 **to exploit** to treat others unfairly for your own purposes, to misuse – 19 **to rape** to force to have sex – 27 **twig** very small thin branch

I had to stop for a moment. I was thinking about Halima clinging on to me and kissing me because she had just had her second good meal in weeks and because I was Mama's daughter. I wiped my eyes with the edge of my scarf.

5 'I know we live far away. I know it's hard to believe that things you do here will change things for people there, but they will. People can give money, yes. That's the easy bit, but we are begging you to give us a future by changing things here. If you don't, we will die. It's that simple. We will die because we will have no way and
10 nowhere to live. So, please, change. Change! Change the way you eat, travel, use water! Change the way you treat nature! Stop wasting stuff and just throwing things away. Try to conserve resources instead of just consuming them as if they'll go on forever. They won't. And keep telling your leaders that you want them to act like they
15 care and act like they understand that there is no Planet B. They need to keep the planet alive for all of us, wherever we are, whoever we are.'

I took the mic away from my lips and hung my head, exhausted. People started to clap. The clapping went on for what seemed like
20 ages. I think I heard Aoife shout, 'Go, Zaynab!', but I couldn't be sure.

I felt faint, as if I hadn't even got the energy to stand up. Someone caught me as I wobbled and dropped my crutch. It was the MP, Mr Fanshawe.

25 'Well, that was some speech!' he said. 'Thank you. I will make sure that charity gets plenty of support from the city. You did a great job for them, people don't really consider the indirect effects of climate change on women and children.'

He shook my hand. The woman from Extinction Rebellion hugged
30 me.

Then, suddenly, my father was there, with Lucas. 'That was very powerful, Zaynab. Your mother would have been very proud of you.'

'And you? Are you proud of me?' I asked, searching his face.

11 **to treat** to behave towards sb/sth in a particular way

Father looked serious. 'I am, of course. But if you are to give a voice to thousands, Zaynab, it is important that you understand how to use the power Allah has given you.'

What did he mean by that?

5 'I need to sit down,' I said. My leg was really beginning to ache.

Mr Reeves came up to us.

'Good job, Zaynab. The whole school will be proud of you. We're all marching through the city now, but I am going to suggest that you take it easy, stay with your father and wait for us to pick you up

10 again later. What do you think?'

I was really sad not to be going with everyone. They looked so happy and so full of energy, but I was exhausted. I couldn't pretend I wasn't.

'I'll stay with her, too,' said Lucas.

15 I couldn't bear for him to miss the real demo, but he was determined not to leave me, so I had to give in.

We were making our way across the square to a café when we heard shouting behind us to please wait. Three men, one with a big black camera on his shoulder, another with a huge fluffy micro-

20 phone on a stick and the third, who was shouting at us, in a suit and tie and a huge, fake-looking smile.

'Here we go!' said Lucas. 'Film crew. Get ready to be famous, Zaynab!'

The man with the big smile and too many teeth stuck his hand

25 out to shake mine.

'James Scott, SouthWest TV.'

'We caught your speech and loved it,' added the man holding the camera.

James grunted. 'Anyway, we'd like to do a bit of an interview.' He

30 looked at Father. 'I assume that's OK?'

'She needs to sit down,' said Lucas, and the crew looked at my leg.

---

5 **to ache** to hurt – 15 **to bear** to take the responsibility for – 16 **to give in** to admit that you are defeated or to agree to do sth that you do not want to – 20 **suit** formal jacket and trousers – 21 **tie** *Krawatte*

'Ooh! Nasty! I guess fighting climate change is a dangerous business!' said James.

I gave him what I hoped was a pitying look. He was embarrassed. Good.

5 He smiled at Lucas and said, 'She wants to sit down? Yeah. No problem. Let us buy you a drink. What do you want? Coffee? Tea?'

'Orange juice, please,' I said, irritated by the way he treated me as if I weren't there, 'and my friend will have a hot chocolate, I expect.'

10 Lucas stuck a thumb up.

'Awesome,' said James, as we squeezed into a small café. 'Can I ask how old you are? Fifteen? Sixteen? And what's your name again?'

'My name is Zaynab and I'm twelve,' I said. 'Thirteen in August.'

'Oh, OK! Really young!' He spoke as if that disqualified my opinion
15 immediately.

'So? I am old enough to know that our planet is being destroyed and there is no Planet B!'

James nodded, but he did not seem to be really listening. 'And where are you from?' he continued.

20 'Yewburton.'

'I mean, originally.'

I had known exactly what he meant, of course, but I was feeling unhelpful and sure that they only wanted to interview me because I looked different.

25 'Somaliland. You may not have heard of it, ours is a country which does not officially exist. At the moment,' I added.

'Interesting, interesting.' He sounded impatient. 'OK, so we'll start filming now, if that's OK with Dad?'

'I am sure my daughter will be glad to tell you about her cause,
30 and the charity her mother worked for,' Father said. He gave me a look which said, 'And nothing else.'

'OK. We'll take that as a yes. So, Zaynab. I am going to ask you a few questions and Pete, here, is going to hold this boom over us.

---

3 **pitying** showing pity as well as a bit of contempt – 14 **to disqualify** *here:* to make sth irrelevant or unsuitable – 29 **cause** aim that sb is fighting for

Just ignore him and ignore Sean on the camera, OK? Just look at me. Looks more natural, then. And your buddy?'

'Lucas.'

'Hi, Lucas. Might talk to you, too, OK? Right, here we go.'

5 He coughed and smiled with all his terrifying teeth on show.

'I'm speaking to some young, *very* young, climate protestors, one of whom has come all the way from Somalia to tell us how we should be dealing with the so-called climate crisis. Tell us about what you are doing here today?'

10 I could feel my blood boiling. 'I'm from SomaliLAND, I am not telling you how to do anything – we ALL need to be doing something and it's not a "so-called" climate crisis ... it IS a climate emergency.'

'Well, I can tell you feel very passionately about this topic! But what do you think it achieves, coming out here, skipping school?

15 Lucas. You look like a sensible chap. What's your take on all this?'

I felt an urge to punch the man. Lucas squeezed my arm.

'You should just interview Zaynab,' Lucas said. 'She's the one who really knows what's happening.'

I could not keep the anger out of my voice when I spoke.

20 'We are here because you and older generations think you can use up the earth and leave us with nothing. We are here because adults have let us down. We are here because we won't take it anymore. You want us to be silent when our futures are being trashed? You want us to be silent as our oceans die and our ice caps

25 melt and the deserts take over while you carry on as if nothing is happening? Well, we won't be silent. We *can't* be silent.'

James smiled again.

'Great! Great! So, Lucas, you're pretty modest about your part in all this, but I expect you and your school have given Zaynab a bit

---

5 **to cough** *husten* – 13 **passionate** [ˈpæʃənət] having strong feelings about sth –
15 **chap** *(inf)* man, boy – 15 **one's take on sth** one's view or opinion on sth – 24 **trashed**
ruined, destroyed – 24 **ice cap** thick layers of ice and snow that cover the North and
South Poles – 25 **to melt** *schmelzen* – 28 **modest** humble, reserved

of a helping hand here. It is a bit of a girl thing, isn't it, this climate stuff, what with Greta being the star. Should we guys feel left out?'

I nearly exploded. Lucas shook his head in disgust and the nasty guy's smile vanished in an instant.

5 'And you, sir?' he said and turned abruptly to Father. 'How do you feel about your daughter being up on a stage and playing truant from school?'

'I am proud of her. I am proud of all these children. But you? You should be ashamed to be interviewing them both in this manner.'

10 'Interview terminated!' said Lucas. 'Bye!'

'Rather defensive, aren't we?' James asked, in an unpleasant tone. 'We're giving you publicity. Isn't that what you want? What you need?'

'No,' I said, firmly. 'What we need is proper reporting on what is 15 going on.'

'I don't think proper reporting is really your thing, is it?' Lucas added.

James waved 'cut' at the cameraman and swept out of the café. The boom man held out his hand.

20 'Sorry about him. Bit of a prat,' he said. 'My kid is taking part today. St Luke's school. I'll make sure there's a decent edit on YouTube or something. Don't think that any version he'd like will be on the local news tonight. Keep it up though. You're doing great.'

'Most people are good people,' said Father, watching them leave.

25 'And most companies?' I asked, challenging him to respond.

He sighed. 'Yes, Zaynab, yes. We have been over this before. Please do not look for problems where there are none. Do you really think I am any less focused on doing the right thing than your mother?'

He pinched my cheek and laughed, turning to Lucas. 'She's like 30 a dog with a bone, sometimes, don't you think?'

Oh, I am … especially when I think the bone might be rotten.

---

11 **defensive** oversensitive – 18 **to sweep out** *here:* to leave quickly – 20 **prat** *(inf)* an incompetent person – 21 **decent** satisfactory, acceptable – 31 **rotten** very poor quality, very bad

LUCAS

Zaynab tried to ring the Jurassic Oil and Gas placard guy several times on the way back to school, but his phone was switched off. She was actually growling with frustration as she repeatedly punched redial.

5 I couldn't help thinking how hard it must be for her dad to know that she didn't trust what he was doing. 'Do you really think your dad would deliberately get involved in something that would be bad for the environment?' I asked in a brief gap between her call attempts.

10 'I never said it was deliberate,' Zaynab replied. 'I just smell a rat.'

I wanted to ask her what mattered more to her – making things better between her and her dad or uncovering bad stuff on his project – but I was frightened of annoying her even more.

I watched her as she kept hitting redial. She was so intense, so
15 focused. Maybe obsessed.

'You think I'm obsessed,' she said, suddenly.

Great! I kept forgetting that she could read my mind!

Before I could say anything, she continued: 'I can't just close my eyes. I can't ignore my instincts. Mama was the same, she would
20 never shrug and say, "Oh, well. Doesn't matter." Never.'

She hit redial again. No luck. She sat back in her seat and closed her eyes. 'Anyway. You're the one who spotted the placard. You're just as obsessed as me,' she said, quietly.

Was I?

25 'What will you do if you discover bad stuff about Jurassic Oil and Gas? Or would you be disappointed if there isn't any?' I asked.

Zaynab opened one eye to look at me sideways.

'Trust me. There'll be bad stuff,' she said. 'It's a fossil fuel business. Burning sunlight, remember?'

---

3 **to growl** to say sth in an angry voice – 8 **gap** break – 10 **to smell a rat** *(idm)* to suspect that sth is wrong *(Verdacht schöpfen)* – 15 **obsessed** too interested or focused on sth

'I know, but if it's going to upset your dad ... Aren't there other things we can investigate?'

She snapped upright.

'No, we have to do this. What's wrong with you, Lucas? Whose
5 side are you on?'

'Yours, of course. I just think your dad is on your side, too.'

She frowned and closed her eyes again. 'We'll see. Now please can you stop talking? Sorry! I'm tired and I want to think about Mama.'

10 When I got home, Dad was stretched out on the sofa, clutching a beer can and with a big packet of crisps in his lap, reading the paper.

'That girl was on TV,' he said, nodding towards the TV. 'She's got some guts, I give the little maid that. Up on a stage with her broken
15 leg and all.'

'She's my best friend,' I replied, hoping that was still true.

Dad looked impassive as he said, 'Yeah, you told me before. I do remember, you know. I'm not daft.'

'*I* went to Exeter today, too,' I added.

20 He grunted. 'Like I said, I'm not daft.' Then he waved towards the garden. 'Got you some seedlings from a customer. Bit of a quid pro quo. I done him a favour, he gave me a few winter veg. Kale, leeks and spinach. See if you've got green fingers.'

And then he was back to the sports pages of the paper,
25 acknowledging my thanks with another wave of a hand.

As I examined the array of plants, I thought about Zaynab and her father. I wanted her to get on with him properly and trust him. Maybe I should try harder with my dad, too?

---

2 **to investigate** to examine sth to try and find out the truth – 11 **lap** *Schoß* –
14 **maid** (*here: dial*) girl or young woman – 17 **impassive** not showing any emotion –
21 **seedling** a very young plant – 21 **quid pro quo** gift that is given to sb in return
for sth – 22 **kale** *Grünkohl* – 23 **to have green fingers** (*idm*) to have a talent for
gardening – 25 **to acknowledge** [ək'nɒlɪʤ] to accept – 26 **to examine** [ɪg'zæmɪn]
to take a close look

ZAYNAB

Lucas's words echoed in my head. Would I be disappointed if Jurassic Oil and Gas turned out to be good guys? Did I want to prove my father wrong more than anything else?

It was so hard to work out what was making me do what I was
5 doing and to work out if it was the right thing. Mama would have known, but I could not ask her. I felt so alone.

I lay on my bed, absentmindedly stroking Toffee, who had fallen asleep by my side. Then Max, the guy with the Jurassic Oil and Gas placard, called. 'Sorry I was a bit unfriendly earlier,' he said. 'What
10 do you want to know?'

'Why are you focusing on Jurassic Oil and Gas?' I asked, cautiously.

'Because they're local. Their headquarters are in London but their operations are based outside Exeter. Because my mum used to work for them and saw some dodgy stuff. Because they are yet another
15 carbon polluter. Simple, really. Why are you interested?'

I wondered how much I should tell him and then decided to take a chance.

'My father is involved with working for one of their projects and I smell a rat. What did your mother see?'

20 'Oh, you know, the usual. Shady deals with nasty governments. Talking the talk without walking the walk. Total rubbish about helping the environment in one place while destroying it in another.'

I could hear that the anger in his voice was tinged with hopelessness.

25 'What sort of shady deals?' I asked.

'Kickbacks for officials selling them exploration rights at rock bottom prices, when they were owned by the people and not theirs to sell. Jobs for princes. Maybe even helping regimes get weapons

---

11 **cautiously** carefully – 14 **dodgy** *(inf)* suspicious *(verdächtig)* – 20 **shady** not honest, illegal – 21 **Talking the talk without walking the walk.** *(idm, inf)* not acting in a way that agrees with the things sb says – 21 **rubbish** *(inf)* nonsense – 26 **kickback** sum of money that is paid to sb illegally – 26 **rock bottom price** very, very cheap

in exchange for oil. I'm still trying to find proof of that. They cover it up really well, but Mum saw stuff. The thing that really gets me is the greenwashing. They basically say, "Hey! Look over here at all our charitable spend and environmental goody-two-shoes stuff!"
5 while they're grabbing land and sinking wells right down the road. It sucks.'

'What happened to your mum?'

'They sacked my mum for asking questions. I'd like to nail them,' he added. 'But she won't help and I can't prove anything.'

10 'Why won't she help?' I asked, disappointed that there didn't seem to be anything concrete.

'Frightened. Scared she'll lose her current job. Worried she'll get labelled as a troublemaker. It's really bad, but that's how it is. I do what I can, but, of course, I get nowhere.'

15 I could visualise his shrug of defeat.

'Anyway, if your dad finds out anything and you want help, I'm here,' Max continued. 'It's hard battling these companies. They have all the time, the money ... and the lawyers, of course.'

'Yes, but we have the passion, determination and energy,' I
20 countered.

He laughed. 'Yeah. You've got that in spades.'

He seemed to be about to hang up, and then he said, 'Are they going to be working in your home country? Find out what they're offering. Look for the catch, look for the bribes and kickbacks.
25 Nothing will be what it seems.'

'Do you mean they'll offer my father a bribe? He would never take one. Never.' As I said it, I knew it was true.

'They'll know that. They do their homework. They've probably hired him because everyone knows he's honest and that gives them

1 **proof** evidence – 4 **charitable** giving to those in need (the homeless, poor etc.) – 8 **to sack** to tell sb that they can no longer work for them, to dismiss – 8 **to nail sb** *(inf)* to catch sb and prove that they have been breaking the law – 12 **current** present, being done now – 21 **in spades** *(inf)* in very large amounts – 24 **catch** hidden problem – 24 **bribe** a sum of money that one person offers to another in order to persuade them to do sth – 29 **to hire** *opp of* to sack, to employ sb to do a particular job

great cover, but there'll be something. Something to sweeten the deal. Something to distract from what's really going on,' Max said. 'Might look like something positive. They're clever ... but then so are you, I think. Trust nothing. That's my advice.'

5   'But can I trust you?' I asked.

'As much as I can trust you. Look, I'll help if I can. Sling stuff my way. Research, digging. I'll do whatever I can, but now I've got to go. Good luck and keep me posted.'

I lay back on my bed, hugging my phone to my chest. It suddenly
10 felt very real and very frightening. What if Father lost his job and could never get another one? And all because of me.

I dug out Mama's scarf from under the pillow and buried my face in it for a few minutes. Then I looked at my watch, half an hour to do some detective work before Father got back from Friday prayers.
15   I crept downstairs and into the study. Deborah was in the garden. Toffee followed me in and curled up at my feet.

I started the computer and went to open Father's emails. Password rejected. I tried again, same thing. I felt my heart sink and a sort of crazy ringing in my ears. He'd changed his password. I checked his
20 search history. Cleared. I rocked back in the chair. Why would he do that?

My phone buzzed and I nearly jumped out of my skin. Lucas.

He sounded very anxious. 'Are we still friends? Are you annoyed with me?'

25   'Father changed his password,' I said, ignoring his question. 'And Max says the company is up to something and his mum lost her job trying to find out about it, and she's too scared to talk about it. *Now* do you see why we have to do this?'

He was silent for what seemed like ages, then he said, 'Maybe it's
30 dangerous.'

'You sound like Izzy. I know you're careful, but I didn't think you were a wimp.'

---

1 **to sweeten the deal** to make sth more attractive – 6 **to sling** *(inf) here:* to give, to send – 7 **to dig** to search – 22 **to jump out of one's skin** *(idm)* to be very startled, surprised – 32 **wimp** *(inf)* sb who is afraid or lacks confidence

I wished I had not said that as soon as the words were out of my mouth. Lucas hung up on me. I stared at the phone screen as the tears began to splash down.

What had I done?

5   Deborah must have heard me crying. She came and knocked on the study door. 'You OK, Zaynab?' she called.

I couldn't stop my sobbing from getting louder and louder.

She came in. 'You don't have to tell me anything,' she said, gently, 'and I know you're missing your mum, but I am always very happy
10 to listen. I won't interfere or judge or influence. I'll just listen, if you want me to.'

She put her hand on my shoulder and something snapped inside. I howled and Deborah wrapped her arms round me and rocked me gently.

15 'It's OK. It's OK,' she said. 'Let it out. Grief comes in waves, doesn't it?'

I wriggled free. 'I'm not crying about Mama. I'm crying about Lucas,' I told her. 'Lucas and I aren't friends anymore and it's my fault. I don't know what to do.'

20 She held my chin in one hand and looked into my eyes. 'I don't believe that for one moment. He's devoted to you, and you to him. Even the best of friends fall out sometimes.'

I studied her face. She looked quite a bit different from when I had first seen her. Her skin was a better colour and she had gained
25 a little weight. 'You're really getting better,' I said slowly. 'You're beginning to look normal.'

She laughed. 'I'll take that as a compliment. Yes, I really am getting better. Now, phone Lucas and sort things out. Never go to bed with a quarrel unresolved, not if you can help it.'

30 When she had gone, I rang Lucas. Three times. On the third attempt, he picked up. He sounded very faint, very down. I felt really bad about what I said and I told him so.

---

10 **to interfere** to get involved – 21 **to be devoted to sb** to care very much for sb –
29 **quarrel** argument, fight

'But I *am* a wimp,' he said, sadly. 'You're right. I'm only able to do what I do because you make me ... not in a bad way,' he added, hurriedly.

'That's not true, and even if it was, think about this. Maybe I am
5 only doing what *I* do because of Mama, but I really want to figure out what's going on, Lucas, and I want to do it with you. Please.'

He was silent for a while.

'OK, I'm in. But can we just have tonight off? I'd really like to watch TV and relax, for a change. Please.' He still sounded unhappy.
10 'It doesn't mean I don't care, I just need a break.'

'That's fine. I understand,' I said, though I wasn't sure I did, really. I just knew it was what he wanted me to say.

I heard him give a sigh of relief.

'Friends?' I added.
15 'Friends. Always.'

We said goodbye and I went back to staring at Father's computer.

How on earth was I going to find out what was happening? Maybe I could guess his new password? I was so engrossed in typing in different options, that I did not notice the door opening.
20 'Try asking, instead of hacking,' Father said, icily. 'You'll save us both a lot of time.'

I slid off the chair and grabbed my crutch.

'Stay,' he said, as if challenging me. 'Ask me whatever you want. There really is no big mystery or conspiracy, I am sorry to disappoint
25 you.'

'I was just doing research for homework,' I said.

I had never point-blank lied to my father before and it felt really, really bad.

He frowned. 'OK. But take this with you and have a read.' He
30 fished out a report from his briefcase. 'I'm trusting you with a confidential document, Zaynab. Please do not betray that trust.'

I took it, stuffed it under my arm and hobbled to the door.

---

18 **engrossed** giving all one's attention to sth – 24 **conspiracy** *Verschwörung* – 27 **point-blank** directly, openly – 31 **to betray** to hurt or disappoint sb

'I thought we were on the same page, Zaynab,' he said.

I shrugged. 'I'll read this and let you know,' I said, as I left the room.

Back upstairs on my bed, I thought about how easy it was to hurt
5 and upset people and how difficult it was to get over it. I knew Lucas and I had sorted things, but it felt like a patch, a patch that could come off again. As for things with Father ... well.

I stared at the moors and watched the colours darken and brighten briefly as the clouds flew past overhead and the sun began
10 to sink beyond the horizon. Everything seemed to be changing. Nothing was fixed. I felt as if my brain were being scrambled.

The only thing that didn't change was missing Mama. I tried to concentrate on my prayers, but I felt as if the sadness would overwhelm me.

15 'I really need you now, Mama!' I whispered. 'I really, really do.'

I waited until I felt my heart slow down and my grief begin to fade into the background again.

I dried my eyes and sat up straight, giving myself a mental shake.

I flicked through the report. '*Project Berberosaurus. Strictly*
20 *confidential.*' There were maps of Yemen, Ethiopia, Somalia and home, and aerial photographs of deserts and mountains, and suggested ad campaigns, each with the slogan, 'Do good, feel good, be good.'

I snorted with derision.

25 Then I came to a page that made my blood run cold. A photo of an emergency drought camp, a crowd of women and children waving at the camera. There, at the front: Idil, Asha and little Halima, smiling wide smiles of joy. The caption read: *'Families express their happiness and gratitude before moving to their new, safe homes,*
30 *funded by Jurassic Oil and Gas.'*

Mama wasn't in the photo. Mama was behind the camera. I knew that for a fact, because I had been right by her side.

---

1 **on the same page** *(idm)* in harmony – 22 **ad** *abbr of* advertisement – 24 **derision** mockery, disrespectful laughter – 25 **to make one's blood run cold** *(idm)* to fill sb with horror – 29 **gratitude** thankfulness

LUCAS

'It's a lovely photo,' I said. 'And it's a good thing that they are going to be moved to proper houses, isn't it? Wouldn't your mum have been pleased?'

Zaynab tossed her head in frustration and banged the report
5 down on the library table.

'That's not the point. Father has given them Mama's photos and they're using them for their propaganda! This photo was taken more than a year ago and they were all smiling and waving at Mama and me because they were so happy to see us. They weren't moving to
10 new houses like it says here. Their families were stuck in that dangerous camp, afraid that the girls might get stolen or raped. It's a lie! And it's a lie that Father has helped them to tell, by using Mama, using her work when she isn't here to put things right.'

We were being watched by other people in the library. I lowered
15 my voice as I tried to calm Zaynab down. 'What if your mum knew? What if she gave her permission for the photo to be used? What if she took it so that it *could* be used? Is it really such a big deal?'

A familiar look of fury passed over Zaynab's face.

'I'm just saying ... don't be angry,' I went on. 'Things are already
20 strained again with your dad. They won't get better if you accuse him of something he hasn't done.'

Zaynab shook her head. 'Look at the caption, it's a lie. And you know what? Father doesn't even realise that I was there or he'd never have let me see it. Anyway, that's not the worst thing. Here, read
25 this.'

She pointed me to a paragraph further into the report. *'The youngest child in the foreground of the picture on p56 is particularly photogenic and should be tracked down. If she now looks too old to have maximum impact, an alternative should be sought, but that's the*
30 *look we want – female, tiny, pretty, with big eyes and a Western look.'*

20 **to accuse sb of sth** to blame sb for sth

148

'That's sick,' I said.

'Remember what Max warned me? Look for the catch? Why does an oil company need a picture of a pretty, little kid? Because their do-goody stuff needs *selling*? *Really*? Or are they doing something else?' Zaynab's eyes flashed with anger.

'Something else, I expect,' I said, 'but how are we going to find out what that is? Can you ask your dad?'

'For goodness' sake, Lucas! Like he's going to tell me,' Zaynab said scornfully. 'No, we have to get to the bottom of this ourselves ... with help from Max and Deborah and anyone else who wants to find out what's really going on.'

As we dashed back to lessons, Mrs Baldwin stopped us in the corridor.

'We've had a call from that charity you spoke about, Zaynab. CrisisAid. They want to do a piece on the school and its involvement in climate change initiatives. You'll be pleased to know that I have agreed. I am also giving consideration to some of the more demanding proposals you made on that list. What do you think of that?'

'Great. Whatever you like,' Zaynab said, hardly looking at Mrs B and rushing on.

'Sounds really, really good,' I said, to placate the head. 'Thank you.'

'Finally,' sighed Mrs Baldwin, theatrically. 'Some appreciation.'

'Cashing in, as usual,' Zaynab said, when I caught up with her.

'No! It's really good if she makes a link with CrisisAid because then she can't go back on the climate stuff,' I said, trying to persuade her to be more positive.

'I suppose so. I'm just tired of all the virtue-signalling,' she replied, sounding tired. 'She's no better than Jurassic, when you think about it.'

I could have argued with her, but I didn't want to shatter what felt like a fragile peace and standing up again for someone she saw as an enemy wasn't going to help.

---

9 **scornfully** in a way that shows you think sb or sth is stupid – 22 **to placate** to calm, to satisfy – 23 **appreciation** respect – 32 **fragile** unstable, weak

ZAYNAB

I sent Max a text asking if his mum knew anything about Jurassic's activities in Somaliland and he responded almost immediately: *'Give me until tomorrow night.'*

Back at Hope Cottage, I began searching through all of Father's papers, being very careful to leave them exactly as I found them. Nothing interesting at all.

I searched Google. Pages and pages of information, all of it boring financial stuff. Then a piece jumped out at me. A blog post from another environmentalist, written six months earlier about an oil company distracting critics by promoting a green initiative which turned out to be meaninglessly small, dwarfed by their polluting activities elsewhere.

I emailed it to Lucas. *Is this what they are doing in Somaliland? Am I on to something? Tell me what you think!*

I cleared my search history and decided to go through my physio exercises outside. My leg was still really painful and the exercises were even worse, but I knew I could not skip them.

Deborah was sitting on the little terrace, watching the sun go down over Honeybag Tor.

'We get beautiful sunsets back home,' I said. 'Unless we have a dust storm, then everything goes dark red. It blots out the sun. You can't go outside, or your lungs will fill up and you'll be suffocated.'

Deborah shivered. 'Terrifying. We don't know how lucky we are, here. Sometimes it's hard to believe that we're heading for mass extinction.'

'It feels much, much more real and more frightening back home because it's already happening,' I replied, trying not to wince as I stretched my leg.

---

11 **dwarfed by** *(idm) in den Schatten gestellt* – 21 **to blot out** to cover – 22 **to suffocate** to die because there is no air to breathe – 27 **to wince** to make a slight movement because of pain

'You're so passionate about climate change, Zaynab, and it's wonderful, but do allow yourself some time for other things, won't you? Even the Extinction Rebellion handbook says we should have some fun. I hope you read that bit.'

5   'There isn't any time for fun,' I said. 'Time is running out.'

'It makes me feel so sad to hear you say that, Zaynab. You're too young to feel that way.'

'Too young? I'm not too young for the truth,' I retorted.

Deborah sighed. 'I know, but you are a bit of an exception, and 10 you had your mum for inspiration. But for others, if it's all about the gloom and doom and the misery, people will just shut their ears. You, me, all of us … we've got to make people feel excited about fighting this almighty battle. That's why everyone was so hyped at the climate strike. It made them feel great. Fun really does have a 15 part to play.'

I nodded, but I wasn't really listening. I was thinking about how on earth I was going to find out what was really going on with Jurassic.

I finished my stretches and we sat in silence for a while, watching 20 the sky as it seemed to go up in flames and then smoulder into darkness. Almost without thinking about it, I had removed my hijab and my hair fell around my shoulders.

'It's lovely to see your hair, Zaynab. It's beautiful. Thank you for feeling able to take your scarf off.'

25   She paused.

'Your father said you were not obliged to wear the hijab in the house, with me. I hoped you might feel comfortable enough to take it off one day.'

Deborah's eyes were shining.

30   'Did your mother wear hijab?' she continued, gently.

I twisted my scarf into a circle and considered what to say.

---

9 **exception** special case – 11 **gloom and doom** (idm) bad news – 13 **almighty** (inf) great, enormous – 20 **to smoulder** to burn slowly

'Mama respected religion and our traditions and she wore the hijab as a sign of that respect. I wear it as a sign of faith and ...' I tailed off.

I could feel Deborah waiting for me to finish.

5 'And because I am proud to be a Somalilander. I am proud of my difference here.'

Deborah smiled. 'Well, I think it's very empowering to be able to celebrate difference. We are all under such pressure to conform. Good for you!'

10 We exchanged smiles and she reached over and patted my hand.

'Now! We could have some hot chocolate, if you like?' Deborah said. 'There's no point waiting up for your father. The train gets in very late.'

I looked at her in surprise. 'Train? Why? Where has he been?'

15 'London. I think he said he had a meeting with a government minister. He probably thought you wouldn't be very interested.'

I stayed quiet. I could feel her watching me, waiting.

'You know, I am very good at listening. And very good at keeping a confidence,' she whispered. 'Just so you know.'

20 She got up and went inside. I followed and sat down at the kitchen table while she boiled milk.

'It's exciting that my dad's seeing a minister. Can you ask him who he saw and what about?' I said, trying to sound as innocent as possible. 'Only, I probably won't see him in the morning and I am 25 actually interested.'

Deborah gave me a strange look. Could I trust her?

'There's an old saying in my country,' I went on. 'Salt looks just like sugar. A woman called Aamiina taught it to Mama. Are you sure that what you are being sold is what the seller says it is?'

30 I watched to see how she would react. Would she understand what I was talking about?

'It's a very wise saying,' Deborah replied, hesitating before adding, 'But sometimes you can just trust the seller, can't you? Just ask them? Is it salt or is it sugar?'

8 **pressure to conform** *Anpassungsdruck* – 19 **confidence** *here:* secret – 23 **innocent** not guilty

I very deliberately didn't reply, but concentrated on stirring my cocoa to make sure none of the chocolate got left at the bottom. Toffee climbed onto my lap and started purring noisily and digging his claws into my thighs as if he was kneading dough. I could sense
5 Deborah watching us both closely.

'He likes you. He has very good instincts, that cat. Do you have good instincts, Zaynab?'

'I think so,' I said, stroking Toffee's plush, ginger fur.

'I think so, too, but sometimes following those instincts can take
10 you to a difficult place,' Deborah said, quietly.

*

That night, I could barely sleep. My conversation with Deborah had been weird – a load of riddles – and now I felt a jumbled mix of fear, excitement and impatience tinged with guilt. Father had asked for
15 my trust and I just could not give it.

What was wrong with me?

4 **to knead dough** to squeeze dough *(Teig)* with your hands so that it becomes smooth – 13 **riddle** puzzle – 14 **impatience** *opp of* patience

LUCAS

Zaynab and I pored over the report again. Apart from the photos, which still made Zaynab's blood boil every time she looked at them, there didn't seem to be anything. Then she got two texts on her phone.

5   The first was from Deborah.

'I didn't have to ask your dad. Google him. D x'

The second was from Max.

'Mum says search Andrew Reece, MP, google his "outside interests" and "follow the money". Mum's too scared to help any further. Sorry.
10 *Stay safe. Trust no one.'*

I typed 'Professor Egal' into the library computer's search engine.

A picture came up from the BBC News website. Zaynab's dad shaking hands with a tall man with dark hair and glasses. There was something creepy about him. His hair was slicked back, his glasses
15 glinted so that you could not really see his eyes, his smile looked fake and his expensive suit looked strangely baggy on his thin frame. He reminded me too much of the horrible journalist who had interviewed us at the protest.

'Look who he's with,' I whispered.

20   Zaynab read the caption. '*Andrew Reece, Minister for Overseas Development, with Professor Liban Egal at a meeting on aid for drought-stricken independent region known as Somaliland.'*

I began to read the article. '*Professor Egal is the local coordinator of a resettlement and planting programme funded by British oil giant,*
25 *Jurassic Oil and Gas and the British Government. Andrew Reece said: "This government is matching funding for this innovative and generous programme which will help those most affected by climate*

---

1 **to pore over** to look at sth very carefully – 14 **creepy** (*inf*) causing fear – 16 **baggy** loose – 16 **frame** body, physique – 22 **stricken** severely affected by sth – 26 **innovative** new and original – 27 **generous** willing to give help, money etc., esp. more than is expected

change. It is good to see fossil fuel companies behaving responsibly and with compassion, countering the pessimistic narrative spread by climate change activists like Extinction Rebellion." Professor Egal echoed his sentiments, saying, *"My research has shown that*
5   *sustainable action on climate change must have the support and active involvement of erstwhile polluters. In this climate emergency, leopards must be allowed to change their spots."'*

'Leopards changing their spots?' Zaynab scoffed. 'He's fallen for their lies.'

10 She pushed her chair back, making the lino floor screech. The librarian gave us an angry look.

'Shhh,' I hissed. 'You'll get us thrown out.'

Zaynab began typing again in the search box. *Andrew Reece outside interests.*

15 I had been wondering what 'outside interests' were. Gardening? Cycling? No. Not hobbies. Businesses. He was a busy man, involved in a whole string of companies from estate agents to breweries.

'What are we looking for, exactly?' I whispered. 'What did Max mean by "follow the money"? And why would we need to stay safe?'

20 We both jumped as Aoife suddenly appeared behind us, slapping us both on the back. 'Hey! You guys! What are we doing next? What are you up to?' she said, pulling up a chair and craning her neck to look at the screen.

I quickly opened a new tab.

25 'Oh, just checking on where the next demo is,' Zaynab replied.

Aoife scrutinised her face. 'Hmmm, that's not what you're doing. Come on, you can trust me! What are you up to?'

I felt myself getting uncomfortably hot. 'Just some research, for homework,' I said, trying to look as bland as I could.

---

2 **compassion** feeling of sympathy and understanding – 2 **narrative** story, report –
6 **erstwhile** former, old – 7 **a leopard can't change his spots** *(idm)* people can't change
their basic nature – 17 **estate agent** company that sells houses and land – 17 **brewery**
['bruːəri] place where beer is made – 22 **to crane one's neck** to stretch one's neck in
order to see sth better – 26 **to scrutinise** ['skruːtɪnaɪz] to examine very carefully

Aoife made a sound like someone spitting out tea. The librarian looked our way again. Aoife continued in an undertone: 'I've never seen two more guilty-looking kids in my life and that includes my little sisters caught in a cupboard with my mum's birthday chocs.
5 So, come on, tell Auntie Aoife what you're doing. Maybe I can help?'

Zaynab shook her head. 'We can't. Honestly, it's for your own safety.'

At this, Aoife laughed uproariously. The librarian stood up and looked ready to come over to our table.

10 'OMG! You guys are a hoot! Do I look like someone who gives a flying flamingo about safety? Come on!'

'We can't,' I said, firmly. 'We really can't.'

'Sorry,' Zaynab added, but Aoife was up on her feet.

'It isn't cool to just drop people, you know. I thought we were all
15 in this climate thing together? But, hey, you want to make it your own little project now you're famous, fine. I get it.'

And with that, she flounced out, glaring at the librarian as she went.

'Tricky,' I said, quietly.

20 'We'll tell everyone when we can,' Zaynab said.

I brought up Andrew Reece's page again. On the fourth page of search results, a detail jumped out. He had been on the board of directors for none other than ... Jurassic Oil and Gas.

'There! Look!' I said, forgetting to keep my voice down.

25 The librarian pointed at the door. Zaynab put her hands together in prayer and mouthed 'Sorry!'

The librarian shook her head and returned to her screen.

'He *was* a company director, but he quit last year,' I said, reading on. 'He isn't involved anymore so that's not it.'

30 But Zaynab was skim-reading as fast as she could. 'He may not be ... but look at this! Mrs Linda Alison *Reece*, his wife, appointed

---

8 **uproariously** in a very noisy way – 10 **to be a hoot** *(idm, inf)* to be very funny –
10 **to give a flying flamingo** *(idm, inf)* to care – 17 **to flounce out** to storm out –
22 **board** group of people that controls and directs a company – 28 **to quit** to leave
(a job), to resign

to the board to replace him. And she owns nearly a million shares in the company. Follow the money!' She looked jubilant.

I scratched my head. 'I don't get it. This doesn't prove they're doing anything wrong, does it? I mean, there's nothing in that project report. It's all charity stuff. They are literally giving money away! It doesn't make any sense.'

'Think about it. Max said there'd be a catch, that this might be a bribe. This is covering up something else, all this do-gooder stuff. I just know it.'

'Maybe the clue is in the name,' I mused.

'Huh?' Zaynab looked at me as if I was mad.

'I mean, I know why they chose a dinosaur name. They're called Jurassic Oil and Gas. But why such a weird one? Have you ever heard of this dinosaur?'

I was frantically googling Berberosaurus as Zaynab pondered the question.

'Found it. "*Fossil remains found in East Africa*" ... Well, that explains *that*,' I said, disappointed.

Zaynab's eyes glinted. 'No, you're on the right lines, Ghost Boy. It is staring us in the face.'

She took over the keyboard and opened a fresh tab. She typed in 'Berbera.'

'That name is actually very cunning. Look.' She pointed at the results. 'Berbera is where a huge new oil pipeline is being built, at the main port.'

'Oh my god! So you think Jurassic will be using that pipeline? That means they must be drilling for oil somewhere nearby!'

'Exactly. The tree-planting and house building is just a cover-up. Why would they be spending all that money if there wasn't something big in it for them? They aren't going to be pumping trees through that pipeline, are they?'

---

1 **shares** *(pl) Aktien* – 2 **jubilant** overjoyed, extremely happy – 15 **frantically** in a hurried and wild way – 23 **cunning** in a clever way by deceiving other people – 25 **port** harbour

She sat back in her chair, arms folded, looking angrier than I'd ever seen her.

'Do you think your dad is really in the dark about all this?' I said, horrified.

5 'I hope so,' Zaynab said. 'I really do, because if he isn't, he's betraying everything Mama stood for and he's betraying me. Us. My people. This is greenwashing and it's Jurassic's speciality, just like Max and that blogger said.'

'Well, let's hope he doesn't know,' I said anxiously.

10 'I hope so, too,' Zaynab said. 'Because what am I going to do if he does?'

ZAYNAB

I was so nervous when I handed back the report to Father that evening that my hands were trembling.

'Why is it called Project Berberosaurus?' I asked, trying to sound casual.

5 Father smiled. 'Jurassic Oil and Gas always choose dinosaur names for their projects. It's pretty obvious why.'

He had answered without a moment's hesitation. Either he did not know, or he was a good liar, or there really was nothing going on. I had to bite my tongue to stop myself saying what I thought the
10 name signified. As Lucas kept reminding me, get the facts straight first.

'So, my jewel. Was there anything other than good news in these pages?' he asked, searching my face.

'No.' I was so tempted to add, 'Not in *these* pages ...'

15 He seemed stuck for something to say.

'Anyway,' I continued in as bright a voice as I could muster, 'I'm off upstairs to do my homework.'

'Don't you want to work in the study? You can use the computer, if you want. I have reading to do, so you won't disturb me.'

20 I could tell his antennae were twitching with suspicion.

'No, it's fine! My tablet will be enough. Thanks!'

Father held up the report. 'I hope you now trust me as much as I trusted you?'

'Trust is earned,' I muttered, hobbling upstairs and into my room
25 as fast as my leg would let me.

Lucas and I had agreed: he was going to write a letter to Mr Fanshawe, the MP who had spoken at the big rally, to ask about

---

2 **to tremble** to shake slightly – 4 **casual** (pretending to be) relaxed – 10 **to signify** to mean, express – 19 **to disturb** to interrupt, to bother – 20 **suspicion** *Verdacht*

overseas aid; and I was going to comb through the online oil surveys and seismic reports.

There was so much material and so much oil and gas still in the ground in my country and our neighbours. Wars and unrest had stopped companies investing, but now companies were sniffing around for opportunities.

None of what I read could be used as evidence to prove that Project Berberosaurus was greenwashing. Part of me felt like giving up. I picked up Mama's scarf and wound it round my neck. Could I still smell her perfume? No, not really.

I scrolled down page after page and then switched to images.

And there it was. A map showing oil reserves across an area that not only included the camp, but also the small forest that Mama had helped to save and the last of the land that was still being farmed by nomads. I clicked on the image and read the text.

'*Wellsite geologists estimate two billion barrels of oil at prospective sites, licensed to Jurassic Oil and Gas.*'

I felt sick. I copied the link over to Lucas. He rang me straight away.

'Well, there you go,' he said, flatly.

'You can't believe my father didn't know, can you?' I asked, quietly. 'Nope, I can't. What are you going to do?'

'Ask him outright,' I said. 'What else can I do?'

'Maybe we are wrong to do this,' Lucas said. 'Your country needs the money. Why shouldn't they sell their oil? Britain has. Everyone else has. Anyone who has oil has got rich. Maybe it's their turn?'

'But it's a scam. Corruption. A British company is making money while it's pretending to do good for my people! My country is being destroyed by the climate emergency and these liars are planting trees while they burn more oil. It's crazy. It's wrong. It's like a fire-starter posing as a firefighter.'

---

1 **to comb** [kəʊm] to search everywhere – 2 **seismic** ['saɪzmɪk] related to or caused by earthquakes – 16 **to estimate** to calculate roughly – 16 **barrel** 159 litres – 16 **prospective** potential, possible – 27 **scam** swindle, illegal trick

I was almost screaming with fury. Lucas was quiet for a moment, giving me time to calm down.

'OK, that's bad, very bad. I was just checking that we are doing the right thing. Let me know how it goes with your dad. I don't envy
5 you,' he said sadly, and hung up.

I copied and pasted the image and article into a document and sent it to print downstairs.

Then I sat, holding my breath, knowing that Father would see the printout as it emerged.
10 After a few moments, I took a deep breath and started to make my way slowly down the stairs, resting on my crutch on almost every step. It felt like the longest walk of my life.

Deborah was just coming out of the kitchen as I reached the bottom stair. 'Zaynab! Are you OK? You look terrible!'
15 'I feel terrible,' I said, turning towards the study. She followed me into the room. Father sat with his head in his hands, the printout on the floor in front of him.

'Sorry,' Deborah said, hurriedly. 'I'll leave you in peace.'

She closed the door behind her and, as she did so, Father looked
20 up. His eyes were red.

'What did I say, Father?' I asked him. 'What's in it for them? Now we see, it's a scam. A con! You know why they really called it Berberosaurus? You know about the oil pipeline being built in Berbera? The fossil fuel pipeline? They'll drive people off the land
25 and then they'll start drilling for oil! "*Look, you poor displaced people! Here are some sweeties. See how kind and generous we are! Now run along while we trash your future for profit.*" You told me this was about planting trees and rebuilding communities, but it's just another filthy cover-up for greedy polluters, isn't it?'
30 'It's what I was told,' Father said, softly.

'And you believed them?' I found myself almost yelling. 'They're going to destroy Mama's trees. They are going to poison our air. They

---

4 **to envy sb** to be jealous of sb – 22 **con** (*inf*) trick – 25 **displaced** forced to move away – 29 **filthy** very dirty – 29 **greedy** selfish, wanting a lot more than you need – 31 **to yell** to shout

are going to speed up our destruction! But you believed them. You believed them because you wanted to make your theories come true!'

'More trees will be planted and the housing will be built. Your
5 mama would be pleased,' he said, refusing to look at me.

'*Pleased*? Mama would never have supported uprooting yet more people, even if they were going to get little brick boxes to live in – especially not near the coast, where it's already completely rammed with people!'

10 He shrugged, uncomfortable under my gaze.

'It's all about the oil, Father. Don't pretend. You used Mama's photo. Your friends would use little Halima to be the face of a scam.'

He looked bewildered.

'That photo of people delighted by their new homes? That's a lie.
15 How do I know? Because I was there, I was by Mama's side. Where were you?'

I could almost see excuses forming in Father's brain. I kept going.

'And the Minister you saw yesterday? He will make money from this! How is that allowed?' I asked.

20 Father look genuinely shocked. So this, this was the killer blow? Not Mama? 'The minister? He's not financially involved!'

I burst out laughing. 'Oh, Father, you are too trusting. His *wife* is a director of Jurassic.'

Father looked stunned.

25 'Yes. A director and a big, big shareholder.'

He put his head in his hands again.

'You have to *do* something,' I said, as forcefully as I could.

Father looked up. 'What can I do? Think of the consequences for our country! We need the revenue from oil. And what if there are
30 consequences for us? For you and me?'

'I don't care. We have to do the right thing. We have to do what Mama would have done!' I could feel tears beginning to run down my cheeks.

8 **rammed** too full – 14 **delighted** very happy – 20 **killer blow** sth that puts a stop to sth – 25 **shareholder** a person who owns shares in a company – 29 **revenue** income, money that is earned

Father stared at me. He looked old, tired, scared. 'Your mama is dead. She is *dead*, Zaynab. Nothing can bring her back. It is just you and me, now. We have to survive. I could be blacklisted as a troublemaker. I may find it impossible to get another job. We may be thrown out of the UK and never be able to go back home, either. Do you have any idea what happens to people who criticise companies and politicians? Nothing good, I can promise you!'

'But we have to do what is right. We must stop this, we must! We can send the story to a newspaper. It's corruption!'

Father groaned. 'Who will be interested in such a story? Everyone in the West believes all of Africa is corrupt.'

'It is *this* British minister who is corrupt! It is this British company which is corrupt! If you won't send this to a newspaper, I will!'

Father held out his hand. 'Please, Zaynab. I forbid you. It is for me to decide.'

But I refused. 'No, we are going to blow this wide open. You can't stop me.'

'Even if it means those camps your mother worked in for so long all stay as they are? Even if it means no safe homes for those women? Think about it! It would be your mama's legacy!'

I felt a flash of anger. How dare he try to pressure me this way? 'Don't, just don't! Did they ever find their fresh, new, cute little kid to promote their death and destruction?'

I snatched up the paper and limped over to the door.

'You're being overdramatic. Don't forget, I trusted you,' Father said.

'And I *tested* you,' I replied. 'And you failed.'

I sent Lucas a text: *'Bad. Very bad. Speak tomorrow.'*

3 **to survive** to manage to get through, to continue to live – 3 **blacklisted** banned, rejected – 20 **legacy** sth that sb leaves when they die – 23 **to promote** to help make sth happen

LUCAS

Zaynab was not on the bus the next morning. She didn't text or phone. Everyone asked me where she was and I couldn't tell them or explain. Even Mrs Baldwin came to find me at breaktime to ask if I knew why she wasn't in school.

5   'I noted Zaynab's absence in assembly. I cannot get any reply from her father,' she said, eyeing me keenly. 'Do you have any information, Lucas? Is she on some escapade I should be aware of? I hope she hasn't asked you to cover up for her.'

'No,' I replied. 'I don't know anything, except that she was fine 10 last night.'

She scrutinised my face. 'Well, in the absence of any news from her father, I expect you to keep me informed. I can rely on you for the truth, Lucas?'

I nodded. 'Of course, Mrs Baldwin.'

15   The truth was that I was worried sick. I had looked everywhere for her, including in the tiny boxroom set aside for her prayers. I'd never been in the room before and it felt like an intrusion, even though there was absolutely nothing to indicate what the space was being used for. I wondered how Zaynab felt, in this tiny room alone. 20 It must have been hard for her to pray properly with her leg in its brace. I lingered for a while, feeling her absence like a pain in my chest.

At lunch, Rudy saw me sitting alone and came over to chat. 'Hey, buddy!' he said. 'You're white as a sheet! I'm beginning to see why 25 Zaynab calls you Ghost Boy. Any news of her?'

'I haven't heard anything.' I checked my phone again as if to prove the point. Nothing.

'That's not like her, is it? I mean, you two are like joined at the hip, aren't you?'

---

11 **to scrutinise** to examine very carefully – 17 **intrusion** act of entering a place where you are not welcome – 21 **to linger** to stay, to hang around

I know I blushed, but Rudy wasn't the sort of boy to make fun of emotions. 'Is there anything I can do?' he asked, kindly. 'Have you fallen out? Want to talk it over?'

I shook my head. 'It's nothing like that.'

5   I was about to tell him. I *wanted* to tell him.

'You can trust me, you know,' Rudy added.

Trust! Everything seemed to be about trust!

Aoife and Jack joined us, followed by Sophie-Ann and the twins. It felt good to have them all around me.

10   'What's occurring?' asked Aoife, jauntily, before picking up on the atmosphere of gloom. 'Where is she, then?' she asked. 'Not back in hospital, I hope.'

I found myself beginning to cry.

'Hey!' Sophie-Ann put an arm around my shoulders. 'I'm sure
15   she's OK! Maybe she's at the hospital, having the brace taken off?'

'No, that's not for another three weeks,' I sobbed.

'Has it got something to do with what you were doing in the library?' Aoife asked. 'Is she in trouble?'

I nodded. 'I think she might be. She might be in big trouble with
20   her dad ...'

And then I just cracked and told them everything. For a moment they just sat there, pretty much with their mouths open in shock.

'We have to rescue her!' Poppy cried.

'She won't need rescuing,' said Rudy. 'She might need time to
25   sort things out with her dad, though.'

'There's no way that's going to get sorted.' Aoife was dismissive. 'He's blown it.'

'He's probably got her locked up!' Daisy was wide-eyed with worry.

'No,' I said, firmly. 'He wouldn't do anything like that. He loves
30   her.'

'Whatever,' Aoife said, standing up and slinging her bag over her shoulder. 'I vote we go up there after school. Sort it out. Agreed?'

---

10 **jaunty** high-spirited, happy – 26 **dismissive** showing that you don't think sb/sth is important or has much value

'OK, OK.' I began to wish I had stayed silent. 'But you can't let on that you know. You really can't. Do you understand? Zaynab would kill me.'

'Rubbish!' said Aoife. 'She knows you're her best friend ever. Stop
5 worrying, kiddo. We'll just make like we're worried she might have repeated her leg-breaking moonlit walk. Chill!'

Easy to say, I thought, as I went off to yet another lesson in which everything would go in one ear and come straight out the other.

5 **kiddo** *(inf)* kid

ZAYNAB

When I woke up, my phone and tablet had gone from my bedside table. There was a note from Father.

'We need to talk.'

I went to the bathroom, took a shower and dragged on my uniform.
5 A leaden feeling of dread had spread through me. Everything was an effort.

He had taken away my phone, taken away my power, taken away my means to contact Lucas. I felt defeated, deflated. All the fire had gone out of me.

10 When I'd struggled downstairs, Deborah was making coffee. She gave me a strange look which I could not interpret. Whose side was she on?

I picked at a piece of toast. It tasted like cardboard.

I didn't turn my head as Father came into the room. He pulled
15 up a chair next to me and laid his hand on my arm.

'I'll be late for school,' I said, taking another bite of the cardboard toast. 'And you're already late for work.'

'I am not going to work and you are not going to school,' he said, quietly.

20 'I want my phone and tablet back. Now,' I said, still refusing to look at him. 'You can't keep me prisoner. Deborah? Are you going to let this happen?'

Deborah looked uncomfortable. 'It's really none of my business, but I'm sure your dad isn't keeping you prisoner and that he
25 wouldn't take your phone.'

I laughed. 'Yeah. Well, he has.'

Father tightened his grip on my arm. 'You can have your phone back when we have talked. Finish your toast and come to the study.'

---

8 **defeated** lost, beaten – 8 **deflated** having lost confidence, hope and optimism –
13 **cardboard** thick, stiff paper – 21 **prisoner** *Gefangene(r)*

He let go of my arm and left.

To her credit, Deborah looked shocked. 'What is going *on* with you two?' she asked. 'You've been so much happier, I thought!'

'Leopards and spots,' I said, getting up from the table. 'Leopards
5 and spots.'

I went into the study and sat in the chair that he had set out for me. 'Is this an interrogation?' I asked, as I sat down. 'Sure feels like one. Except I should be interrogating you, not the other way around.'

'Such a drama queen, sometimes! Where is the respect?' he asked.
10 'Respect? I don't know. You tell me,' I muttered.

He tried a different tone. 'Please, my jewel. Listen to what I have to say, it's important.'

'Go ahead,' I said.

He looked haggard, as if he had not slept. I felt a twinge of pity.
15 'We have not been seeing eye to eye,' he began.

I could not stop myself retorting, 'No kidding.'

'Please, please. This is not easy for me ... or for you, I know.' He took a deep breath. 'I have made a very bad mistake, but I cannot let you make it worse. That is why I took your tech. You are like your
20 mother ... impulsive, combative. It is good, sometimes. It works, sometimes. But now is not the time.'

I had already heard enough. 'So! We just let this happen? We turn a blind eye? We do it your way by being nice to these *thieves*? It's corruption. It's a betrayal of all Mama's work. It's a betrayal of me
25 and my friends, fighting for climate justice. It's a betrayal of little Halima and her sisters!'

He nodded. 'I know, I know. Please, hear me out. We cannot send this to the press, I know what will happen – it will be buried, I will be fired. The project will go ahead.'
30 'You can't know that!' I said, angrily.

---

7 **interrogation** questioning – 14 **haggard** tired – 15 **to see eye to eye** (*idm*) to agree –
16 **kidding** (*inf*) joking – 19 **tech** *abbr of* technology; *here*: mobile phone – 20 **combative**
eager to fight – 22 **to turn a blind eye** (*idm*) to pretend not to notice sth – 24 **betrayal**
an action which is disloyal to sb – 28 **to bury** *here:* to cover, to forget

'I can, I do. This man, Mr Reece, he is well-connected. The story will be buried.'

'So what do we do? Nothing?' My anger was growing.

'There is another way. I have a plan. I've been awake all night
5 thinking about it. I need to put this right, whatever the personal cost.'

I was suspicious. 'Why should I trust you? A leopard cannot change its spots, whatever you say. I feel like I don't even know you! What would Mama think about all this? Would she agree with what
10 you've done?'

'I loved your mama more than I can ever say, but even we argued about the best way to go about things. I thought I was going to prove that my way is the better way. In this case, I was wrong. I am sorry.'

He took a long pause and blew his nose, noisily.

15 'Even now, I admit, it is hard to turn my back on the good things this project would have accomplished, but you have shown me the error of my ways. The corruption of that minister? That finally opened my eyes to things I have been choosing not to see, and you are right. It must be shown for what it is. A trick. A fraud.' He took
20 my face in his hands. 'Can you forgive me? I beg you to forgive me! Can you do that?'

'That depends,' I said, guardedly. 'That depends on your plan.'

He cleared his throat and began: 'Project Berberosaurus launches in three weeks, with a reception at the Natural History Museum,
25 which is famous for its dinosaur fossils. You can see why they chose the venue. The minister, the directors and the media will all be there. I will be giving a speech, outlining the benefits for our country ...'

He took a deep breath before continuing, his voice sounded broken.

30 'Instead, I will reveal their true intent. I will tell the world about the corruption. I expect it will mean the end of my career, but I can see no other way. They won't be able to silence me in a public place,

6 **cost** *here:* damage, loss – 16 **to accomplish** to succeed in doing – 23 **to launch**
to start – 24 **reception** formal party to celebrate a special event – 26 **venue** place,
location – 30 **to reveal** to make known – 30 **intent** intention, plan

even if they try to stop the cameras from rolling, the story will be out, and my conscience will be clear.'

He carried on speaking but I was no longer listening. Yes, it was a plan, and it would probably work, but I had a much, much better plan ... one which Father would never support, but which I would carry out if it was the last thing I ever did. For now, I needed to play along and give him no clue that I thought his idea was anything other than brilliant.

2 **conscience** ['kɒnʃəns] a person's moral sense of right and wrong (*Gewissen*)

LUCAS

It felt very strange walking to Hope Cottage with Aoife, Rudy and the others.

Aoife was in war-mode, striding down the track purposefully. If I had let her, she would have battered down the front door.

5 Deborah saw us from over the garden wall. She was smiling and looked better than I'd seen her for ages. 'Wow! Look at you all!' she said. 'What a lovely surprise!'

'We've come for Zaynab,' said Aoife.

'To rescue her!' piped up Poppy.

10 Deborah gave us a quizzical look.

'Don't think she needs rescuing, unless you know something that I don't. She's with her father on the moors. They won't have gone far because of her leg, but I think they just carried on down the track. Should be easy to find them.'

15 As we turned to go, she took me gently by the shoulder. 'Can we have a quick word, Lucas?' she whispered.

'Go on,' I told the others. 'I'll catch you up.'

They dumped their bags in the cottage and set off towards the moors.

20 'You must have been very worried about her,' Deborah said, kindly. 'But she does not need rescuing. Not anymore.'

'What's happened?' I asked. 'Last text I had from her was late last night, she said everything was bad. Very bad.'

'I imagine it was, but things are different now.' Deborah said. 'She
25 and—'

I interrupted, 'She could have told me she was OK. It's been a nightmare!'

I was beginning to feel really hurt and angry. Zaynab must have known I'd be worried. Why couldn't she have sent me a message?

---

3 **purposeful** determined, resolute – 4 **to batter down** to hit sth so hard that it falls to pieces

Instead, she'd gone swanning off on the moors, *my* moors, without me.

'It's been tense. Very, very tense, Lucas. I am sure you know why. Those two have had a lot of sorting out to do. There's a lot of grief, a lot of guilt and a lot of baggage, but I think they're making amazing progress. You know Zaynab would never upset you if she could possibly avoid it. You're incredibly important to her. You know that.'

'Do I?' I said, and I could hear the sullen tone in my voice.

'Course you do! Don't be silly!' she ruffled my hair. 'Go on … catch up with your friends. She'll be pleased to see them, I'm sure, but you're the one who will make her day.'

By the time I got to the bottom of the lane, the others were on their way back, picking their way over the close-cropped turf, watched by some sheep. Both Zaynab and Liban looked exhausted, but Zaynab's face lit up when she saw me.

'Lucas!'

She tried to hobble/run towards me, leaving Liban with Aoife and the others.

'Woah!' I shouted, running to meet her. 'Careful!'

'We're going to get them!' she whispered urgently in my ear as she embraced me. 'We're going to be all over the news. I can't wait to tell you all about it!'

I felt a stab of jealousy. She'd made a plan without my help. She hadn't needed me. She hadn't communicated with me.

As usual, she read my expression accurately. She took my hand. 'Listen. None of this would be possible without you. Don't be a grump! We're going to really *do* something for the planet, for my people. You and me.'

'And your dad?' I asked. 'You told me it was bad. Very bad. It was the last thing I heard from you. We thought he was keeping you prisoner, punishing you.'

---

5 **baggage** emotional issues – 8 **sullen** cross, moody – 11 **to make sb's day** *(idm, inf)* to make sb very happy – 21 **to embrace** to put your arms around sb – 27 **grump** *(inf)* a bad-tempered person

She squeezed my hand tightly. 'He took my phone, you see. I know that sounds bad, but it's been more like *me* punishing *him*. It's not completely good now, but it's better. I am so sorry that I did not text you when I got my phone back. It's been full-on with Father,
5 we've had a lot to talk about.'

I kicked at some loose stones on the track.

'Please, Lucas. Forgive me?'

It was very difficult to stay cross with her. 'Nothing to forgive,' I said, returning the squeeze. 'Anyway, I'm the one in trouble, really.
10 I told the others everything.'

'Doesn't matter. They are part of the plan,' Zaynab explained. 'We're going to blow this whole thing wide open.'

'Is your dad helping?'

Zaynab was absolutely buzzing with excitement. 'Yes, but not in
15 the way he thinks he is. He's got his plan, but I've got a better one. A much, much better one.'

The others were catching us up. Aoife, Rudy and Liban seemed to be having a lively debate.

'Can't tell you anything right now,' Zaynab whispered. 'But it'll
20 blow your mind.'

4 **full-on** (*inf*) extremely intense

LUCAS

'Your dad is going to go mental when you rock up in the middle of that event,' I said, after Zaynab had talked me through her plan. 'Absolutely mental!'

Zaynab shook her head. 'No, he won't. It's perfect. It saves him 5 from getting into trouble, but we get to be the bad guys! Genius, huh?'

My head was spinning. I had so many unanswered questions. How were we going to get to London? How were we even going to get hold of enough money to get there? How were we going to skip 10 school when Mrs B was already watching Zaynab like a hawk? How were we going to get into the reception? There was bound to be loads of security! What if we got arrested? What if we got stopped before we even got in the room? What if they stopped Zaynab from speaking?

15 Zaynab sat back in her chair and waggled her finger at me. 'You're worrying too much, Ghost Boy. This is our big chance in so many ways. We have to grab it.'

'If a lot of us vanish, Mrs B might send the police after us! We might get expelled.' I felt angry with myself that one negative thought 20 after another kept coming into my head, but I couldn't help it. 'Sorry! I just can't help worrying about these things.'

Zaynab banged on the desk. 'Actually, it's good. We have to plan for ways to stop things going wrong. That's why we are a good team: I think of what can go right, and you think of what can go wrong.' 25 She smiled at me. 'Come on, let's go over it all again, then we can tell the others.'

'You won't like this, but I think it would be better if we got some adults involved,' I said. 'Like Deborah and Extinction Rebellion.'

Zaynab pulled a face.

---

1 to rock up (*inf*) to arrive unannounced

I went on. 'I know it's more exciting if it's just our group, but think about it. If there are lots of us, especially adults, it'll be more like an official protest. It'll get more attention and we'll be sort of hidden in the crowd until the moment comes ...'

5 I watched the idea slowly take hold of Zaynab.

'You're right, we need numbers, presence. It must be impossible for the world to ignore us. And look, it's a museum full of dead creatures ... extinct, fossilised, mummified, stuffed ... we should stage a die-in! A die-in, while a fossil fuel company tries to accelerate
10 mass extinction. What do you think?'

Zaynab was now a ball of energy, crackling with ideas and impatience – an irresistible force.

'Now that *is* genius,' I said. 'Absolute genius.'

She smiled at me, an intense almost crazy smile. 'Did I ever tell
15 you that you are my best friend ever?'

12 **irresistible** inevitable, that cannot be stopped

ZAYNAB

The more I thought about it, the more I knew that Lucas was right about us needing real numbers at the die-in. As soon as I got home, I looked for Deborah in the garden, where she seemed to be chopping all the plants down to stumps.

5 'Hi, Zaynab!' she said, catching my look of horror. 'I'm just cutting everything back, ready for the winter. It looks a bit brutal, doesn't it, but it'll mean better growth next year. How was your day?'

'It was fine.' I didn't want to waste time on small talk. 'I need your help. Can we go inside, please? I'm a bit cold.'

10 'It is beginning to get a bit nippy, isn't it?' she said, packing away her tools. 'Let's have some tea and you can tell me what you want.'

In the kitchen, Toffee was stretched out along the bottom of the range, his tummy pressed against its warm surface and his head back, eyes closed, as if he were in absolute heaven. He took a swipe

15 at Deborah as she leaned over him to put the kettle on the hob.

'Laziest cat in the universe!' she laughed. 'What a life, eh? Twenty-three hours asleep. Oh, to be a cat!'

'I've got too much to do to be a cat,' I said, bending down with difficulty to stroke him.

20 'I know, we all have. It scares me sometimes.' She looked pensive for a moment or two. 'Come on, then. I'm intrigued.'

I told her about Jurassic and the deception we had uncovered. She listened intently.

'I kind of picked up bits and pieces of this already,' she said, as
25 she poured the tea. 'I couldn't help hearing some of your conversations with your father. Sorry, hard not to in a small cottage. It's a tough one, isn't it? You must feel very conflicted.'

---

10 **nippy** (inf) chilly, rather cold – 15 **kettle** pot for boiling water – 15 **hob** Herdplatte –
20 **pensive** thoughtful – 22 **deception** trick, the act of hiding the truth – 24 **bits and pieces** (idm) small parts – 27 **conflicted** worried because you are unable to decide between opposing feelings

'I don't feel conflicted at all,' I said. 'We want the world to know what they're doing. We just need more people to get involved. We want to stage a die-in when Jurassic launch this fake project. Do you think Extinction Rebellion would get involved? Lucas suggested
5 it.'

Deborah smiled. 'It's short notice, but we are set up to take direct action, so, yes. I think I can speak for my group. I'll get in touch with headquarters, too. You'll have no shortage of people in London who will be keen to take part.'

10 She studied my face closely for a few moments.

'Will your father know? Is he OK with this? That's my only reservation. I think that the protest itself is entirely valid and justifiable, but I, personally, would feel uncomfortable if it meant driving a wedge between you two.'

15 'He doesn't know and I ... we ... can't tell him. He's stressed and busy and focused on dealing with what Lucas and I have found out.'

I looked at her, anxiously, trying to be sure that she would not wreck our plans.

'It would be worse for him if he *did* know, actually. It would put
20 *him* in a difficult position with them. Jurassic, that is,' I added, feeling rather pleased with this reason.

'Are you trying to tell me that ignorance is bliss, by any chance?' she replied, with a hint of mischief. 'Well, on this occasion, you are probably right. We'll keep it to ourselves. Now, don't you have some
25 homework to do – and your physio?'

I pulled a face. 'Grrrr! I'm so sick of those exercises and I'm sick of being in pain!'

'I know how you feel,' Deborah said, quietly. 'But it will come to an end. Your leg will get better and you'll be glad you looked after
30 it properly.'

'Sorry,' I said. 'That was thoughtless of me, you've had it far worse.'

---

12 **reservation** doubt, feeling of being unsure – 12 **valid** important – 23 **hint** *here*: very small amount – 23 **mischief** slight naughtiness – 23 **occasion** particular event

And poor Mama worse still. I felt a stab in my heart as I realised that I had not really thought about her for a few days now.

Deborah smiled and took my hand in hers. 'You're a brave young woman, Zaynab, and your mum would be extremely proud of you, I'm sure.'

She got up to put our mugs in the sink.

'And thank you. Thank you for involving Extinction Rebellion. We are stronger together, aren't we?'

'Definitely,' I said, momentarily distracted by a new powerful idea that had come into my head.

'There's just one more thing. Do you think you could get the Red Rebels to come? I don't know why, but I need them to be there. For me.'

'I'll do my best,' she said. 'I'd like them there, too. Their presence makes things very, very special.'

Before I knew what I was doing, I was giving her a hug and she was giving me one back.

We stayed like that for a few minutes and then Toffee tried to join in and we separated, laughing. And crying a bit, too.

'Well, we both have work to do!' Deborah said, briskly, wiping her eyes. 'I'm going to send an email to the Red Rebels right now! We might even have an answer by the time you've finished your homework.'

I went to the study and got out my maths –transformations. How appropriate.

Before I made a start on the worksheet, I sent Lucas a text.

'*Deborah's in. She says we are stronger together.*'

Quick as a flash, a text came back. A ghost emoji and a green heart.

---

6 **sink** *Spülbecken* – 20 **briskly** quickly – 25 **appropriate** right or fitting in the situation

ZAYNAB

The last days of November and first week of December were difficult
and exhilarating at the same time. Father had no inkling of what I
was planning or that Deborah was involved. He was concentrating
too hard on trying to appear normal, while rehearsing what he
5 planned to say. He practised his speech over and over. As I helped
him make changes, I was thinking, 'You'll never have to give this
speech. I'm going to save you.'

He had no idea.

Aoife and the others were amazing. Rudy and the twins had told
10 their parents about the die-in and sworn them to secrecy. The twins'
dad had insisted on buying our train tickets, which was a huge relief
to Lucas, in particular.

We met every break to go over the plans.

'I feel like a secret agent! It's so exciting!' said Daisy, one lunchtime.
15 'Is that what you want to be?' asked Rudy. 'Because I want to be
an investigative journalist and break the stories no one else will
cover.'

'She'll never be a spy!' Poppy laughed. 'She can't keep quiet for
two seconds and she's crap at hiding!'
20 'Undercover cop for me,' said Aoife. 'I love a good stakeout.'

We all laughed.

'You are literally the last person on earth I could imagine
becoming a police officer,' Rudy said, summing up exactly how we
all felt.
25 'Shows how little you know me!' Aoife said defiantly. 'It'd be the
ultimate rebellion. Think about it!'

'Think you've been watching too many cop shows!' Sophie-Ann
said, poking her in the ribs.

---

2 **exhilarating** [ɪgˈzɪləreɪtɪŋ] making you feel very happy and excited – 2 **to have an
inkling of sth** to have a vague idea, suspicion – 19 **to be crap at sth** (*inf*) to be bad at
sth – 20 **cop** police officer – 20 **stakeout** *Observierung*

'What about you, Zaynab? Politics?' Rudy asked.

I hesitated. In the middle of all the excitement, the stark realities of our world suddenly hit me hard. 'We have to secure a future first, don't we?' I said. 'How can any of us make long-term plans?'

5 'Woah! Downer!' Aoife punched me in the arm. 'You, girl, are going to make damn sure we have a future!'

I think we were giving off secrecy vibes because Mrs Baldwin summoned me to her office for the zillionth time. 'I've been watching you, young lady,' she said, narrowing her eyes as she scanned my
10 face. 'And I cannot help but feel that you are up to something.'

I stared back, keeping my face as impassive as possible. I was so lucky I did not blush like Lucas.

'I'm waiting,' she said. 'Anything you want to tell me?'

'Not that I can think of right now,' I said, cheerily. 'But thanks for
15 asking.'

She glared at me and sighed deeply.

'We have come a long way, Zaynab. We have considered and even implemented some new climate-related initiatives – the daily bulletins, for example. And, of course, we supported your attendance
20 at the rally last month.'

I managed to stop myself from snorting at the idea of Mrs B supporting me.

'And yet, I still get the distinct impression that you are determined to do things your own way and behind closed doors.'

25 She didn't seem to expect me to say anything, so I just sat and stared at her until she cracked and looked away.

'If I find that you are planning something, *anything*, that will impact on this school or the attendance record of any of its pupils, then there will be consequences. Do you understand me?'

30 I really wanted to say that sometimes the price is worth paying, but one lesson I have learned is that keeping quiet is sometimes for the best, so I nodded and asked if I could go.

---

2 **stark** harsh, unpleasant – 8 **to summon sb** to order sb to come to you – 23 **distinct** very clear

She waved her hand dismissively. 'Go. But remember what I have said, Zaynab, your way of doing things is by no means necessarily the best.'

Lucas was waiting for me down the corridor. 'Is she on to us?' he asked, casually. I noticed that he didn't seem to be as nervous as he used to be. Only a while back he'd have been terrified to think that Mrs B even suspected, but it seemed a new, braver Lucas was emerging.

Without waiting for an answer, he continued, 'Look what I got from the drama department. Blood capsules! Now all we have to do is come up with something that looks like oil.'

'You're the artist!' I said. 'Surely you can come up with some paint?'

Lucas grinned. 'Leave it with me.'

Back at the cottage, both Father and I were becoming restless. He had told Deborah about the situation so that she would not think he was being rude or irritable because of something she had done. Father thought that I was on edge because I was anxious about him and it made him happy that I cared. I couldn't tell him the real reason.

Three days before J-Day, as we called it, he said at breakfast, 'We've been tipped-off about a big Extinction Rebellion protest on Wednesday. Have either of you got anything to do with this?'

Deborah and I looked as if it were news to us, too.

'It will be a distraction,' he said, irritably. 'I am about to expose a possible misuse of public funds and an important greenwashing story. The arrest of a load of protestors may steal the headlines and the real story will get buried.'

'I'm confident the Jurassic story will be far, far bigger,' I said, as reassuringly as I could; but I felt sick. What if I were wrong?

---

1 **dismissively** contemptuously, in an insulting way – 15 **restless** impatient, worried –
17 **irritable** bad-tempered, cross – 18 **on edge** nervous – 22 **to tip-off** to warn

On J-Day minus two, I had to go back to hospital. Father sat in the waiting room, drinking cup after cup of coffee. I asked if I could sit up and watch while the surgeon unscrewed my brace.

'External fixator,' he said, correcting me. 'If you want, it's not that
5 exciting and it's a bit easier for me if you stay lying down. But you have to promise me something in return. You must, must, must do all the physiotherapy exercises or you will end up with a wonky leg. Understand? And you're still going to need these.' He pointed at my crutches.

10 I was extremely disappointed, I had banked on ditching them.

'I must be able to walk, even run, without them by Wednesday,' I said. 'It's really important.'

He burst out laughing. 'Wednesday? *This* Wednesday? Not a chance, young lady! Not a chance!'

15 He carried on chuckling as he worked. Ordinarily I would have found it fascinating to watch him take out the bolts, but it hurt like mad and I wanted to scratch the holes so badly when he was done. He wouldn't let me and before I could disobey, a nurse put dressings on them.

20 My leg was like a stick. All the muscles had withered away. Even I could see I would not be able to run about. I just wanted to cry. How stupid had I been to go out on the moors like that! What if I couldn't carry out our plan?

Then I felt a pang as I recalled little Halima's painfully thin limbs.
25 She had walked seventy kilometres with her mother and sister in search of food. If she could do that, surely I could manage a few stairs at the museum. I gave myself a mental kick up the backside and grabbed my crutches.

'No if onlys,' I muttered under my breath. 'No if onlys.'

---

3 **surgeon** ['sɜːdʒən] *Chirurg(in)* – 7 **wonky** *(inf)* unsteady or not straight – 10 **to bank on sth** to rely on – 10 **to ditch** *(sl)* to get rid of – 15 **ordinarily** usually, in general – 18 **dressing** bandage, plaster – 20 **to wither** to become weaker, to shrink

LUCAS

J-Day arrived. I hardly slept at all, I kept waking up to check my alarm in case it had gone off without me realising.

I showered and got dressed. I had a thumping headache and my throat was sore. I couldn't be ill, today of all days. I just couldn't.

5 I checked my backpack. Squeezy bottle of diluted black acrylic paint. Check. White sheet for my shroud (bought in a charity shop for 50p). Check. Train tickets.

Train tickets. Where were the train tickets? I could have sworn I'd put them in the bag as soon as the twins had given them to me, 10 but they had vanished. I felt sick. I remembered thinking at the time, *Put them in an envelope, Lucas. They might get lost.* Why was I such an idiot?

Perhaps they were in my coat. Dad was in the bathroom and Mum was already downstairs, getting breakfast ready. I caught a glimpse 15 of myself in the mirror at the bottom of the stairs. I wouldn't need any white face paint, that was for sure.

I put my bag down and started searching through my coat pockets. Nothing.

'This isn't happening!' I muttered, feeling a wave of nausea rush 20 over me. I turned back to my bag and tipped the contents out on the hall floor.

I was really trying to be quiet, but I just couldn't help moaning with frustration and disbelief.

I was stuffing the sheet back into my bag as Mum came out of 25 the kitchen. 'Whatever is the matter, Lucas?' she asked. 'You look as white as a sheet! Have you lost something?'

The sheet thing would have been funny if I wasn't so stressed.

I flung the bag towards the stairs and slumped against the wall, putting my head in my hands.

6 **shroud** *Totenhemd* – 14 **glimpse** short look – 19 **nausea** ['nɔːsiə] feeling of sickness

'What is it, lovey? Is there anything I can do to help?' Mum put an arm round me.

'What's wrong with the boy?' Dad said, as he stomped down the stairs. Before I could stop him, he had trodden heavily on my bag, which he then kicked to one side. 'Your mum has told you and your sister a million times. Don't leave your stuff lying around.'

I barely heard him. I was watching a thin trickle of black paint ooze out from the zip. Dad followed my gaze.

'What the hell have you got in there?' he said, grabbing the bag and ripping it open. He pulled out the sheet, which was now covered in paint.

Mum shrieked, 'Don't get that mess everywhere! For goodness' sake, Lucas! What is this about? Is this for an art project?'

By this time I was having a meltdown. Everything that could go wrong, had gone wrong. I tucked my knees up to my chin, made myself as small as I could and howled.

Dad threw my bag and the sheet out of the front door and then he pulled me to my feet.

'You'd better clean up this mess, sharpish,' he said, roughly. 'And then you've got some explaining to do.'

'But I'll miss the bus!' I wailed. 'I have to catch the bus!'

'You'll miss breakfast, is what you'll miss, my lad,' Dad said. 'Now get cleaning.'

Mum helped me wipe up the paint, which had got splattered and flicked all over the place. Most of it came off without a problem, but some of it left a dark mark. Mum put her finger on her lips and winked at me, trying to reassure me that it didn't matter. I put the sheet in the bin and took everything else out of my bag. My water bottle was OK and so was my pencil case. Better still, my sketchbook was dry and undamaged. From its pages fluttered two small pieces of orange and cream card. The train tickets.

I stared at them in disbelief. I honestly didn't know whether to laugh or cry.

---

7 **trickle** drop, dribble – 8 **to ooze** to flow or leak out slowly – 14 **meltdown** (*inf*) *Nervenzusammenbruch* – 21 **to wail** to cry, to weep

'What you got there?' asked Dad, 'You going somewhere?'

I looked up at the clock. Even if I left right then and there, I'd never make it to the bus in time.

I'd failed Zaynab. I had failed my friends. I had failed myself. I sat down at the kitchen table and began to cry again.

Dad had picked up the tickets. 'Seems our lad is off to London for the day!'

'London? Are you going to London? Today?' Mum asked, anxiously. 'I don't remember anything about any school trip? Have I missed a permission slip?'

'Where'd he get the money, is what I should like to know! We need some answers when he can stop blubbing,' Dad said, flinging the tickets back down on the table and grabbing a slice of toast. 'And what's with all the paint and the sheet?'

I don't know why, but I suddenly thought, *What the hell.* This was meant to be the most important day in my life so far and now I'd blown it, so what did I have to lose?

'One of the parents bought all our tickets. A group of us were going to London to protest about an oil company who are doing some disgusting things in Zaynab's country and it was going to be a huge story. A mass die-in with us in shrouds.' I choked back fresh tears. 'It *will* still be a big story, but I won't be part of it, not now that it's all gone wrong. I've missed the bus, so I've missed the train.'

I got up to go to my room so that I could text Zaynab and tell her how sorry I was. I had no idea what I would do then.

'Wait!' said Mum. 'You could still catch the train. There's time ... if Dad takes you.'

Dad practically spat out his toast.

'And why would I do that?' he asked.

'Because this really matters to him. Can't you see that? We should be proud of him! He could be like other kids and spend his life on his phone or computer, but he's not, our son is trying to make a difference. He needs our help.'

'And how is going to London in a sheet covered in black paint going to make a difference?' Dad asked.

'Because we are going to do something that will be in the news, all over the media. Honestly, Dad, if you knew what this company was doing, how it's lying and cheating and how a politician is making money out of it, you'd be as mad about it as I am. It's disgusting.
5 They'll be killing people with what they plan to do, they have to be stopped. And there'll be hundreds there and I'm meant to be one of them,' I said. 'Please, Dad! I can't miss this, I just can't!'

'So,' he said, slowly. 'A bunch of kids are going to stick it to the man? Is that what you're saying?'

10 I nodded. 'Yes, and some adults, we're all going to stick it to the man.'

He thought for a while before asking, 'And you reckon it'll be on TV?'

I nodded, holding my breath.

15 He banged his hand down on the table.

'You know what? Great. Give the billionaires what for! I like it! Mind you make sure the TV people get your name right!'

Mum looked pleased and then worried. 'Just one thing ... is it Extinction Rebellion? Will you be safe? I don't want you tasered or
20 sprayed with tear gas or anything. I saw what happened to those people on Waterloo Bridge!'

'Don't worry, Mum,' I said, trying to sound a lot calmer than I felt. 'I'll be safe, we've got it all worked out.'

'Better get our skates on!' Dad said. 'Here, Megan. Get the boy a
25 sheet and let's see what we can save of that paint.'

My phone buzzed. Zaynab. *'Where are you? I am panicking here!'*

'On my way. See you on the train. Sorry', I texted back.

'Better be a good excuse', came her response.

Oh, it was!

30 Dad didn't say much as we roared around the back roads to Exeter but when we pulled up outside the station, he handed me some money and said, 'Don't die on an empty stomach. Have a burger on me. A veggie burger, if you must.'

---

19 **to taser** *mit einem Elektroschocker angreifen* – 20 **tear gas** *Tränengas* – 24 **to get one's skates on** *(idm, inf)* to hurry

'Thank you, Dad,' I said. I felt almost overwhelmed by emotion. 'Thank you.'

I wanted to say 'Jazakallah,' as Zaynab did, to really express how much this meant to me, but I held back. He already looked a bit
5 embarrassed as he mumbled, 'Yeah, well, I don't need your mother giving me a hard time. You can cook me a ham and leek pie at the weekend, maybe. Those leeks you've been growing are looking good.'

I grinned. 'Maybe cheese and leek?'

'Get on with you!' he snorted. 'I'm not driving you to bloomin'
10 London if you miss that train.'

Zaynab was waiting for me by the ticket barrier. Her eyes were red but she beamed a massive smile when she saw me.

'Don't *ever* do that to me again!' she said, walloping me with her crutch. 'I mean it!'

15 Rudy's mum, Mrs Harris, was waiting with Deborah and a group of other people from Extinction Rebellion. She had Kitty with her, who was dressed up in a skeleton costume, her bright eyes shining out of blackened sockets.

'There's no way Rudy and I can go on an XR protest on our own.
20 Sorry! Kits will stay with me –' at this, Kitty stuck out her tongue and stamped her foot – 'Kits will *probably* stay with me. She's an old hand at these things, now, but I'll make sure she isn't a pain.'

Kitty stuck out her tongue. 'But I am going to be a pain. I am going to be a pain to the bad people!'

25 Zaynab high-fived her and then turned to me.

'We're really going to do this,' she said, squeezing my hand. 'We're really going to do it!'

6 **ham and leek pie** *Schinken-Lauch-Pastete* – 9 **bloomin'** *(inf)* damned – 22 **to be a pain** *(idm)* to be annoying

ZAYNAB

I felt a crazy kind of calm as we emerged from the Tube at South Kensington. I stood on my own for a moment, staring up at the building with its towers and arches built of bricks the colour of desert sand. I felt as if I had been waiting for this moment for ever
5   and Mama was right by my side. I felt a hand on my shoulder and I turned to see a woman, face as white as bone and as impassive as a statue's, dressed in long, red, flowing robes.
'You came!' I whispered. 'You're really here!'
The woman seemed to smile with her eyes and then joined her
10   comrades in the Red Rebel Brigade as they made their slow stately way up the steps to the museum entrance, arms outstretched, palms upturned.
I think I nearly lost it at that moment. I felt overcome with emotion. Lucas stood beside me.
15   'Wow. They're something else, aren't they? I feel like we are part of something enormous, global ...'
His voice trailed off and I saw that he was near to tears, too.
'We are,' I said. 'Come on, we've a job to do.'

Once in the building we had to go through security. The guards on
20   duty smiled but said nothing as they rummaged amongst the sheets and water bottles in our bags. Kitty had already plastered herself with white face paint and danced around in front of the guards, waving her arms about and wailing. One of them pretended to be terrified of her, which she absolutely loved.
25   Beyond the ticket desk, I could see a vast hall, like something out of Harry Potter. People in shrouds were already gathering and the Red Rebels were processing slowly around the gallery on the upper

---

3 **arch** *Bogen* – 7 **robe** piece of clothing that covers all of the body – 10 **stately** impressive, majestic – 11 **palm** *Handfläche* – 20 **to rummage** to search

floor. Above them, a huge recreation of the skeleton of a prehistoric monster hung from the ceiling, a dinosaur from the sea with huge fins.

'Ichthyosaur,' whispered Lucas. 'Mary Anning found the first one
5 when she was our age, two hundred years ago, on the ... guess what ... Jurassic coast!'

It felt like an omen.

Deborah and Mrs Harris got us all in a group in the cloakroom and turned our faces a deathly white with a tub of face paint and a
10 sponge and then helped us to pin our sheets so that they would not slip. I wished I didn't still need my crutch because I had to wear my sheet like a Roman toga and it did not look nearly so sinister, but Aoife said I looked like a statue in a graveyard and that was fine.

Protestors kept arriving all the time as we made our way to the
15 Great Hall, and there was a buzz of excitement that grew and grew. Outside, a camera crew were assembling their kit and two police officers were talking to security.

Deborah tapped me on the shoulder. 'Well done, Zaynab. We reckon we'll have about two hundred here and kids from at least
20 three other schools. It's going to be a great demo, very impactful, but peaceful and serene. You should be very proud of yourself.'

I wondered if I should have told her exactly what Lucas and I planned to do. But no, we could not risk anyone trying to stop us. What we were planning wasn't going to be exactly peaceful or serene.

---

7 **omen** sign, warning – 12 **sinister** frightening – 13 **graveyard** place where dead people are buried – 21 **serene** calm and quiet

LUCAS

I lay on the smooth marble floor of the Natural History Museum, staring up through the bones of the giant 3D model of the ichthyosaur. It was as extinct as humankind would be if we didn't do something soon. I was playing dead, but my heart was beating as fast as a hummingbird's wings.

Around me, a sea of bodies covered in sheets, with only their whitened faces visible. Eyes closed. Barely breathing.

There was an eerie silence. It made me think of the stillness and quiet on the moors before a storm blew in. Only we were the storm, this time.

I felt fear and elation as we waited, waited, waited. Surely people could hear my heart, which thumped wildly underneath the bag of paint taped to my chest?

Zaynab lay next to me, her bony elbow sticking into my side, her crutch propped against my leg.

'You won't chicken out, will you?' she hissed under her breath. 'Promise! Promise me you are in!'

I turned my head towards her. She had asked me this a million times. Nothing had changed. She fixed me with her fierce stare and my heart stopped for a moment.

'Well?'

I nodded.

'I'm in. I promise.'

She moved her elbow just enough to stop my ribs hurting. We closed our eyes and got back to the die-in.

In a few minutes, we'd die again and wake the world up.

Oh yes.

ZAYNAB

I'd set the alarm on my phone and lay there, waiting for it to go off.
The wait seemed to last an eternity. All I could hear was the
swooshing of blood in my ears and the jump thump of my heart.
What if I couldn't get up with my crutches? What if guards tried to
5 stop me as I climbed the great stairs?

There was nothing to be done now. What would be, would be.

Lucas lay next to me, eyes closed. Aoife was on my other side,
breathing slowly and deeply.

I felt as if I could not get enough oxygen in my lungs.

10 Suddenly, Mama's face came into my head once again and I heard
her voice as clearly as if she were right beside me.

'*Be brave, my daughter. Be brave, for me and for your country.*'

I felt a tear roll down my cheek and imagined it carving a little
rivulet through the white make-up. I must have looked crazy. Maybe
15 even frightening.

My phone buzzed against my hip. My heart went crazy, it felt as
if it might jump out of my mouth.

I prodded Lucas gently with my crutch. He sprang into action
and, pulling me upright, we began picking our way across the bodies.
20 Aoife began to rouse the others, who would follow on a few minutes
after us.

'Are you sure you know exactly where we are going?' Lucas asked
me and I pulled out the map that I'd grabbed at the entrance.

'We should have practised this!' he said, in dismay. 'It's two floors
25 up!'

I pulled at my shroud, covering my face almost completely. 'Come
on, before the guards spot where we are going.'

'We're drawing too much attention!' Lucas said as we made our
way towards the stairs.

---

2 **eternity** a very long time, forever – 14 **rivulet** small stream – 18 **to prod** to push sb
with a finger – 24 **dismay** feeling of fear, worry

People were pointing at us, staring at us. A couple of demonstrators got up and started to follow us. We pushed past people coming the other way.

'We'll have to go faster. Can you do that, Zaynab?' Lucas's voice
5 was urgent, scared.

'Take the lift, if you want to go upstairs,' a woman said. 'It's just there. And good for you, great demo!'

I smiled my thanks and caught Lucas's raised eyebrows.

'I know! I should have seen that on the map!' I hissed.

10 A couple of guards began to make their way towards us. They looked friendly enough, but it was clear they were going to ask us where we were going. The loos were in the opposite direction so that excuse wasn't going to work.

Suddenly Mrs Harris appeared with Kitty and stood between the
15 guards and us. Kitty began her wild dancing and cavorted up to the guards, darting round them like a mischievous spirit, with Mrs Harris apologising and laughing and distracting them.

'Praise be to Allah for the gift of Kitty!' I managed to say, as I hobbled along as fast as I could.

20 The lift was there, waiting. A man with a toddler was about to get in, but stepped aside when he saw us. The small child began to cry loudly.

'You're a bit scary!' said the man. 'But I guess that's how you're meant to be!'

25 'Sorry!' Lucas said as we bundled into the lift. He pressed 2 and the doors closed.

I leaned against the wall of the lift. 'I think I might faint,' I said.

'You? Faint?' Lucas laughed, nervously. 'Never! Give me the map. We need to get this right straight away, we won't get a second chance.'

30 The lift pinged. We stumbled out and turned away from the main hall and down a corridor. Ahead of us, a thick red rope hanging from two poles blocked our way. A man in a dark suit wearing an

---

15 **to cavort** to jump or dance around excitedly – 16 **mischievous** ['mɪstʃɪvəs] slightly bad, naughty – 31 **rope** *Seil*

earpiece stood on the other side. He shook a finger at us. 'Private function. Please go back the way you came.'

I pulled at Lucas and made him turn with me.

'What are you doing?' he hissed. 'We have to go that way! There's no other way in!'

'I know, I just needed a moment. When I say run, run!'

I waited, ready to swing round on my crutches.

'Run!'

I walloped a pole with my crutch and the whole thing topped over. We ran past the man, who started to shout into his walkie talkie as he lunged for us. I whacked his shin with my crutch and he yelped in pain.

'Sorry!' I said, as we charged down towards the open door.

Two more men appeared, blocking our way. They grabbed at us and missed as we ducked and swerved, too fast for them to catch us.

We burst into the room, a large, high-ceilinged space with Jurassic's logo hanging on the walls and tables covered in white cloths and laden with fancy food. Men in suits and women in smart dresses everywhere. Five men and a woman sat at a long table set up along one wall under a giant TV screen showing a film of Somaliland children playing and laughing. Each of the people at the table had a microphone in front of them and a camera crew seemed to be getting ready to film.

Everyone stopped what they were doing to stare at us. I think some were shouting at us to stop, but all I could hear was a rushing in my ears as if I was underwater.

Then I heard Lucas yell, 'Speak, Zaynab! Tell them why we're here!'

Ahead of me, a group of people had stopped talking, stopped drinking. They stared at me in horror and disbelief. I couldn't see Father anywhere.

---

11 **to lunge** to run quickly after – 11 **to whack** *(inf)* to hit hard – 11 **shin** Schienbein –
19 **smart** chic, fashionable

'You are liars! You are liars and cheats! I know what you're planning! I know the truth about Project Berberosaurus,' I bellowed. 'You pretend to be doing good for Somaliland, for the planet, but you are only interested in one thing – money! You will kill us all for money! You will take away my future, all the children's future, for money!'

A man stepped in front of me and grabbed my shoulders.

'No!' I screamed. 'No! You can't stop me! You can't! Let me go!' I twisted violently and wriggled free, stumbling towards the top table. Tears of fury and frustration were pouring down my cheeks.

The man I recognised as Andrew Reece, the MP, stood up and started to back away. I rounded on him. 'You! You are corrupt! A thief!'

'Well, well! That's quite a greeting, young lady. Listen, I think you're in the wrong place. Your people are downstairs, doing their die-in thing ... which I think is admirable, by the way. I am a great champion of the environment, myself, and that is why you've picked the wrong company to attack. We are the good guys.'

He looked round the room as if expecting to be clapped.

'The *good* guys!' I scoffed. 'You've got a pretty twisted idea of what is *good*!'

His face darkened to a beetroot red.

'I am really not sure what you think you are playing at,' he began, 'but I think it's time for you to go now.'

'What *I* am playing at?' I laughed. 'I am not playing at being a public servant. I am not playing at being a friend to poor countries. I am not playing at being a friend to the planet.'

Through the haze of tears, I suddenly made out Father, making his way towards me. I put my hand up, trying to tell him to stay back.

I was dimly aware of a growing volume of noise behind me and of Lucas shouting, 'Quick, quick! Now! Zaynab! Now!'

---

20 **twisted** sick, corrupt – 22 **beetroot** *Rote Beete* – 31 **dimly** not clearly, slightly

'But, you know what? If the world is as you say it is, as you would have it be, then you may as well get it over with,' I screamed. 'You're ending our lives, killing our futures. You may as well kill me now!' I smashed my hand against my chest and felt the fake blood bag
5 burst.

A great bloom of scarlet spread across my white shroud and started puddling at my feet. I let myself fall to the floor as if in slow motion. As I lay there, for a split second, the mad energy vanished. Everything went incredibly silent and calm. I almost felt as if I had
10 actually died.

Suddenly, a familiar voice pierced my cocoon of silence. Father. Urgent, desperate, distraught. Immediately, I could hear screaming in the background, somewhere very far, far away. And then the noise was back properly. Screaming and shouting.
15 Deafening. Terrifying.

I closed my eyes. Father was urging me, 'Stay with me. Stay with me, Zaynab!'

---

11 **to pierce** *here:* to penetrate, to be able to be heard – 12 **distraught** [dɪˈstrɔːt] very upset

LUCAS

When she burst her blood bag and fell to the ground, it was mind-blowing. Everyone gasped or screamed. She looked as if she had really been shot. The red just spread across her like a poppy opening in the sun. For a moment, I could believe that she was dying and I
5   felt a terrible pain. I realised I was holding my breath. I think everyone was. It was as if time was slowing right down, everything was happening in slow motion.

Then a sound came out of me, as if I was a wild animal caught in a trap.

10 I ran to her side and began to pour the black paint in a great circle round her, so that it started to drift into the red. As I did so, I chanted, 'Oil is death. Blood is life. Oil is death. Blood is life'. I hadn't planned to do any of this, but it just felt right. A sort of calm spread through me as I became completely absorbed in my chanting and creating
15 a work of art. I was only jolted out of my trance by Liban, as he pushed me aside and dropped to his knees beside Zaynab.

It was like someone had suddenly jacked up the volume on a sound system. There was a kind of deafening hubbub. People screaming, calling for help, calling for calm. A camera flashed. Lots
20 of cameras flashed. Someone was asking me questions, but I just couldn't focus on what they were saying. The room was spinning. I felt sick. I felt exhilarated. I felt crazy. We had done it!

Liban was holding Zaynab close to him, whispering to her and stroking her face. As the crowd pushed forward, he ordered everyone
25 to stand back and give her some air.

Andrew Reece and his security guy took this as a chance to get out of the room, but Aoife and the others blocked their way.

'You're going nowhere, Sunshine,' said Aoife. 'Let's all hear what you've been up to, eh?'

3 **poppy** Mohnblume

Rudy was filming on his mobile and he wasn't the only one. Everyone had their phones out, taking pictures or videos. The minister looked like a rabbit in the headlights.

'Get out of my way!' he shouted, almost hysterically. 'Get these kids out of my way. Arrest them!'

He began to push, but Aoife and the others just stood strong, smiling.

'Aw! You do realise the world is watching you make a tit of yourself? But, sure, assault a minor, why don't you?'

He threw up his hands in desperation and then sat down heavily on a chair and started pulling at his tie.

He looked defeated and I felt grimly proud of what we'd done.

---

9 **to assault** to attack – 9 **minor** child, teenager – 10 **desperation** feeling you have when you are in a very bad situation

ZAYNAB

I could vaguely hear someone calling for help while another voice was urging everyone to calm down.

Father had gathered me up in his arms and kissed my face, soaking me in his tears and rocking me against his smart suit, now
5 covered in white face paint. 'My jewel. My precious jewel. What have they done to you?'

I slowly opened my eyes and grinned up at him. 'Nothing! Absolutely nothing! Fake blood! See?'

I dipped my fingers in the red and held them up to his face.

10 He growled at me and held me more tightly. 'You will be the death of me, Zaynab, but I could not be prouder of you. Your mama would be so proud, too. Come on, let's get you up. Can you stand?'

I had forgotten all about my leg, but now it was throbbing with pain. Father lifted me and I stood on my good leg, gazing around
15 me.

A wave of nausea washed over me as Father and Lucas helped me up. I clung to them both while the craziness raged all around me. Then I looked down and saw the circle of black that had bled into the patch of red and back up at Lucas.

20 'Did we do OK?' I asked him.

'Not bad,' he said, smiling. 'I think they noticed!'

Father was shaking his head in disbelief. 'You two, you've nearly given me a heart attack! You know that? But, why? You know I had promised to tell the truth!'

25 'I had to come. *I* had to do it,' I said. 'I couldn't let you sacrifice your job.'

A young man squeezed through the throng and pointed his phone at me.

'Daniel Cooper. *Guardian*. I am live streaming you. Can we do
30 an interview? Are you well enough?'

27 **throng** crowd

I stood up straighter and suddenly the pain from my leg threatened to make me faint. For a moment, I hung between Father and Lucas like a rag doll, but then I pulled myself up and faced Daniel's camera.

'Everyone knows that the planet is in danger, but some people
5 still believe that making money is more important than saving Earth. People like these men, here.'

'I am not going to take any lectures from a load of out-of-control kids!' the Minister spluttered, getting up from his chair. His tone had changed completely. He positively snarled at me, 'Why don't
10 you just go back to that great unwashed rabble of do-gooders downstairs? Because I have news for you, all of you. In the real world, real decisions have to be taken, we can't all skip around and knit our own lunches, you know. There's no magic money tree. There are no easy answers.'

15 'How dare you!' I said and I could hear the venom in my voice. 'How dare you! You are a thief! Corrupt! Unfit for office! Tell them about your wife! Tell them about her shares in Jurassic Oil and Gas! Tell them about your plans to get even richer from our oil, while you pose as a saint! Tell them how it's all a cover-up! A greenwashing
20 scam!'

Daniel pointed his phone at the Minister.

'These are very serious allegations. What have you got to say?' he asked. 'Are they true?'

'Of course not! There's no proof, no proof at all!' he shouted. 'My
25 wife has shares, but that's her business! Totally irrelevant! This is a perfectly legitimate scheme, good for the environment and you people should get behind it, instead of making up stories for which you have no proof!'

'No proof of what?' Father retorted. 'No proof of your financial
30 involvement in a greenwashing scam? No proof that you –' he turned to the Jurassic Oil men – 'no proof that you are exploiting my people, conning them? Oh, I rather think that there is!'

---

3 **rag doll** soft doll made of cloth – 10 **rabble** crowd of noisy people who seem likely to cause trouble – 15 **venom** hate – 22 **allegation** statement saying that sb has done sth wrong – 26 **legitimate** legal

'Project Berberosaurus. It's all there,' I said defiantly, holding the Minister's gaze. He looked as if he might explode with fury.

'You should be ashamed. You should all be ashamed.' Lucas's voice was hoarse from shouting. 'We kids shouldn't have to fight
5 for our futures like this. We shouldn't have to be the ones to show you for the criminals you are!'

'What was that plan again?' I repeated, as loudly as I could, though my voice was beginning to go, too. 'Move people off the land and cram them into shanty towns? Plant a few trees to make yourselves
10 feel good and then drill for oil. You are liars and hypocrites!'

Aoife whooped. 'Go, Zaynab! No more coal! No more oil! Leave the carbon in the soil!' and the others joined in. Reece's security guy seized the opportunity to bundle him out of the room, pursued by the journalist, Daniel.

15 And then more police arrived and started escorting people out of the building. We got caught up in a sort of wave that carried us out of the room. It was a struggle to peel away and get to the lift but, somehow, we managed and had a few weird seconds of silence as the lift descended. Then we were back in the wave, with Deborah,
20 Aoife and the others. We all walked out of the museum together, chanting as loudly as we could.

But if the Minister's aides thought he had had enough bad publicity for one day, they were in for a shock ...

As we stepped out into the sunlight, a great roar went up. The
25 steps of the museum were crowded with what looked like a whole army of photographers and camera crews, all clamouring for me to speak to them. A police officer began to try to clear a path, but no one would budge. He shrugged and turned to me. 'Better give them what they want,' he said, half smiling. 'Only way to make them go
30 away.'

So I stood on the steps and spoke again, telling them all about how Lucas and I had discovered what Jurassic Oil and Gas were

---

4 **hoarse** rough – 9 **shanty** small and unsafe house made of materials such as wood, cardboard or metal – 13 **to seize** to grab, to take – 13 **to pursue** to follow – 15 **to escort** to take sb somewhere – 26 **to clamour** to shout

really up to and how Andrew Reece had helped them along because his wife had shares in the company.

'But this isn't just about money and corruption,' I finished. 'This is about what happens to our planet and to us, the children who are inheriting the mess you've all helped to make. This is about consequences. You want oil and petrol here, you want to fly where you like, holiday where you like? OK. But who pays? Who pays as you burn sunlight? Poor people. *My* people. We pay. Women and girls, in particular. We pay. Rape, trafficking, slavery, exploitation. These are all consequences of climate injustice. You carry on with your pollution and we pay the heaviest price of all – we pay with our lives.'

I pulled Lucas to my side. 'Please, speak.' I whispered. 'Please.'

Lucas drew back his shoulders and took a deep breath. 'I'm just a kid from Devon.' He waved towards Aoife and the others. 'We are all just kids from Devon and we're probably going to be fine. We won't starve. We won't be without water. We can all go to school, get an education, maybe even get a job. We might have fifty years before it really hits us where we live. But I don't want to be someone who didn't care enough to do anything right now. And I don't want to live in a world where my best friend could die years before I do. So, I'm doing something. We all need to do something before it's too late.'

I began to feel the adrenaline drain out of me and the pain and exhaustion flood in. I looked around for Deborah and Mrs Harris and suddenly Kitty was at my side, pulling at my sleeve.

'Look, Zaynab! The red people are watching you!'

There, on the grass at the bottom of the steps, stood the Red Rebel Brigade, hands outstretched, faces impassive, their eyes fixed on me. Then they all bowed their heads for a few seconds before turning and making their slow, dignified way back out onto the street and away.

I felt as if my heart would burst.

---

5 **to inherit** [ɪn'herɪt] *here:* to be forced to deal with a problem or situation that was caused by sb else before – 9 **trafficking** act of selling people or forcing them to do work – 9 **slavery** Sklaverei – 31 **dignified** impressive

LUCAS

We crashed out on the train, exhausted. I was dimly aware of Kitty bouncing around, high on Coca Cola and chocolates, and Aoife and Jack snogging in a window seat.

We were met at the station by Bea the cabbie *and* my dad, scrapping over who would get to drive us all home.

'I've come for the professor,' said Bea, stoutly. 'He's my customer!'

'And this is my son and his best friend!' retorted Dad.

In the end they did a deal and Dad took me and Zaynab, and Bea took Liban and Deborah.

'She's never had a celeb in her cab!' joked Dad, as we climbed the hill to the moors. 'But I got the famous ones, eh? Good on you, little maid! You're all over the TV! Right little firecracker, in'um?'

At Hope Cottage, Liban came to carry Zaynab from the car. 'My precious jewel. Warrior princess!' he said, as he gathered her up.

'She certainly is a little warrior, bless her,' said Dad, gruffly. 'She's done for that politician good and proper. He'll be gone by the morning, I shouldn't wonder! Come and sit up front, Lucas. Best get you home, your mum will have had about a hundred litters of kittens by now!'

As soon as we walked in the door, Mum started crying. She held me ever so tightly, rocking me as if I was a baby. After what seemed like ages, she let me go.

'I am so proud of you,' she said, crumpling up a very wet hanky. 'So proud.'

'Yer mum's been watching the news on repeat,' Dad told me. 'Seen it all a dozen times!'

'I thought that blood was real. Makes my heart stop every time I see her with it all over her chest! They said it was fake, but I still

3 **to snog** *(inf)* to kiss – 5 **to scrap** *(inf)* to fight – 6 **stout** resolute – 15 **gruff** rough and low – 23 **hanky** *(inf)* handkerchief *(Taschentuch)*

found myself thinking that someone had actually shot her!' Mum
said. 'And then you! My own boy! Speaking out like that! On TV!'
    She hugged me tightly again, tears streaming down her face.
    'The boy done good,' said Dad, a slight crack in his voice. 'What
5 did you think, Lara? That was some speech he made, weren't it?'
    'Yeah. He was amazing. Awesome. Incredible. Outstanding ...'
Lara reeled off the adjectives in a bored voice. Then she came over
and gave me a big hug. 'I'm so proud of you, little bro. You are
actually truly awesome. I mean it.'
10   'Did you really get past them guards without them catching up
to you?' Dad asked. 'Never had you down as an athlete!'
    'They could have shot you, too!' Mum said, trying to wipe her
eyes with her sleeve. 'I mean really shot you!'
    'That's what everyone said,' I teased her. 'Even me!'
15   Dad gave me an odd look. 'Yes, well, no more frights for your
mother and me, eh? Planet or no planet. Let's have a bit of calm,
shall we?'
    A bit of calm sounded good to me.

7 **to reel off** to say a long list of things

ZAYNAB

The next few days were crazy. I was interviewed over and over again. The picture of me, covered in blood, dangling between Father and Lucas, went viral. The newspaper headlines screamed 'Blood on His Hands' and 'Minister Resigns in Die-In Drama' Lucas's mum said
5 they sold out of every copy within an hour of the shop opening. Daniel from the *Guardian* sent me his article, which concentrated more on the facts of the greenwashing scandal, but the paper had given the whole of page two over to reproduce what Lucas and I had said. The pictures weren't great. Lucas said he and I looked like
10 we had been to a very bad Halloween party, but that didn't matter.

Mrs Baldwin gave an interview for the local TV company and said that she had not been at all surprised to see pupils of her school splashed across the media. '*We have a culture of activism, here,*' she said. I couldn't be bothered to set the record straight, but Aoife took
15 to saying, 'Culture of activism, my arse' every time Mrs Baldwin was close by. That gave us all a good laugh.

Then I got a message from my old school. I felt a pang of homesickness as I looked at the familiar long, low buildings, painted cream with blue windows and red tin roofs, and the throng of boys
20 in their white tops and blue trousers and girls in white hijabs and blue dresses. Smiling black and brown faces. My people.

They were holding a sheet with a message painted on it.

ZAYNAB is our VOICE
Now the world will listen!

14 **to set the record straight** *(idm)* to correct an error or misunderstanding – 15 **my arse** *(inf)* as if

'That is your achievement, my daughter!' Father said, proudly, as he looked at the picture. 'You have brought hope of real change.'

'And Lucas,' I said. 'I could not have done it without him.'

I felt a pang as I thought about the time when I would no longer have Lucas at my side. That time was coming fast. Too fast.

I found myself unable to focus. I had no energy, no 'oomph', as Deborah described it. The prospect of going home, leaving Lucas and my friends was becoming more real by the day.

That weekend, I just lay about on the sofa, stroking Toffee until he got bored and bit me.

Father came in with a letter addressed to me. The Jurassic Oil and Gas logo was stamped on the corner of the stiff cream envelope.

I tore it open and read the letter. They had a nerve! I wanted to throw it straight in the paper recycling.

'Well?' asked Father. 'What does it say?'

I handed it to him. 'Read it yourself. Seems they want free advice from Lucas and me. Exploitation is their speciality! Oh ... and they want you to come, too. Guess they don't want unaccompanied kids!'

'No, Zaynab, you've got it wrong. They are according you both huge respect. They want to get your advice on what changes to make. You have to take this opportunity otherwise your protest will have been for nothing.'

'Wasn't for nothing, was it?' I said, annoyed by his suggestion. 'We got rid of Reece. We exposed the scam!'

Father nodded. 'Yes, and that was the right punishment for them, but now you have a chance to do something positive. I urge you, please, to take it.'

'I'm not helping them to look good,' I said, irritably. 'How likely are they to really listen to a word Lucas or I say?'

'Only one way to find out,' Father said. 'I am hoping to hear about my own position, too. Not that it will form any part of these discussions, I am sure. I'll ring the school as you'll miss yet another day, unfortunately.'

---

18 **unaccompanied** alone – 19 **to accord** to show, to give

I wondered how many more absences Mrs B would tolerate before she finally went ballistic, but when I saw her at school on Monday, she was surprisingly relaxed.

'It seems you are being given the chance to make a very real
5 impact on this company, Zaynab. I hope they listen to your advice and act upon it.'

It was absolutely the kindest thing she had ever said to me.

'It's the kindest thing she has ever said to anyone!' Lucas said, when I told him. 'Wow. I doubt anything that happens at Jurassic
10 will top that!'

So, we set off on our second trip to London in a week, only this time we had first class tickets. I had been going to refuse this extravagance, but Lucas begged me not to.

'I have never travelled first class!' he said. 'And I probably will
15 never ever have another chance. Please!'

It was nice, I must admit. Father sat a way away from us so that we could talk freely and we luxuriated in the deep seats and drank more hot chocolate than was really good for us.

We were met at Paddington by Jurassic Oil's very own chauffeur
20 called Colin and whisked away in a very smart black car.

'It's electric, miss. But I expect your dad told you. It was the first thing he asked me when I picked him up first time.' Colin winked at me in his mirror. 'I seen you on the TV. Fair shook 'em up, you did! Never liked that Reece character. Dodgy bloke with a dodgy
25 missus. Good riddance, I say! Don't you agree, Prof?'

Father smiled, then he leaned towards me and whispered, 'Colin talks all the time. He's a good man, but indiscreet!'

The car pulled up in front of a huge building made of black glass. It sent a shudder down my spine. Lucas and I exchanged looks and
30 I realised that I was feeling nervous and so was he.

---

2 **to go ballistic** (*inf*) to suddenly become very angry – 20 **to whisk** to rush – 25 **good riddance** said to express that you are pleased that sb has left – 29 **shudder** shiver, shake – 29 **spine** *Wirbelsäule*

We were escorted into a grand room with a long, oval table at which five men and a woman sat. There were three empty chairs at one end.

I was beginning to feel angry at how intimidating the set-up was,
5 like we were being made to feel small and insignificant at one end of the table, while the people the other end had all the power. To my surprise they all leaped up and rushed over to shake our hands and welcome us.

One man, who seemed to be in charge, picked up two of the chairs
10 and moved them right next to his. 'That's better,' he said, smiling warmly. 'I hope we can all feel that we are on the same team.'

'Really?' I said, scornfully, and the man's smile wavered.

'Can I just start by saying how sorry we are?' he said. 'I and my fellow directors ... the remaining directors, that is. We've kicked out
15 a few after last week.'

I remained impassive.

'I'm William, newly-appointed Chair of this board, and these are my colleagues.'

They introduced themselves. I had to admit that they were friendly.
20 'I do not need to tell you that we have made some very serious errors of judgement,' William said.

'You're right there,' I said.

'We want to make some changes,' he said and his expression was intense, focused. 'Proper changes. We thought you might like to tell
25 us what you would like us to do. Please, speak frankly. Don't hold back.'

'I don't think Zaynab ever holds back,' Lucas said, shyly. 'That's why she's so good.'

'Exactly!' smiled William. 'So ... Zaynab?'
30 I took a moment to think and then I said: 'Stop looking for fossil fuels. Stop drilling for fossil fuels. Stop processing and selling fossil fuels. Immediately. Just do renewables. Nothing else.'

---

4 **intimidating** frightening – 12 **to waver** to become less – 21 **error of judgment** wrong or bad decision – 32 **renewables** *(pl)* natural energy sources such as wind, water and sunlight

William's smile faded a little. He glanced at his colleagues before speaking.

'I agree with that, in principle. I think you're right, we all need to move away from fossil fuels. The "immediately" bit gives us a 5 problem. It will take our industry time to migrate our businesses over entirely to renewables, we have obligations to our employees and our customers. We need to invest heavily in new technologies, it cannot happen overnight.'

'But you've been warned about what's happening for years! It's 10 not like this is new!' The disgust in Lucas's voice was unmissable.

'I know, I know. You're frustrated, impatient. You're right, we should have gone further and faster ages ago, but we are where we are. So how about this? We work on a plan to fast-track our move from a fossil fuel company to a renewables company? How does 15 that sound?'

I shrugged. 'It's a step in the right direction, I guess. Depends what you mean by fast-track? We haven't got long.'

'You are right, again, Zaynab. We've been giving serious thought to how we can achieve what is a very ambitious goal. We'll aim to 20 be completely carbon neutral within five years. That's going to be a very tough ask for us, but I think we can and must commit to that.'

His colleagues nodded their agreement.

'But will you promise to stop Project Berberosaurus now?' I asked. 'The drilling bit of it?'

25 'I am glad you raised that,' he said. 'We are pledging the money and resources for the new housing and the tree planting and we will never exercise our drilling licence. We'll keep hold of it, though, to stop anyone else having a go. How's that?'

Lucas and I looked at each other. It was really difficult to hide our 30 excitement and delight, but I wasn't finished with them, yet.

'It's good,' I said, calmly. 'But I need two more things from you.'

The directors looked at me expectantly.

---

5 **to migrate** to change from one thing to another – 6 **employee** worker – 21 **to commit oneself to sth** to say that you will definitely do sth – 25 **to pledge** to make a serious promise

'Firstly, I want you to build the homes where the camps are and a water treatment plant, a school and a hospital and train the staff.'

William smiled. 'OK. That's quite a lot of things in one thing, but, in principle, yes. Go on.'

'And two, help to fund CrisisAid. My mama was a volunteer for them.'

'Not a problem. In fact, we've already made them our charity of choice. Thank you! Thank you, both of you.'

Another idea suddenly came into my head.

'Err ... can I make it three things?'

William and the other directors laughed.

'Your daughter is quite something, Professor!' William said. 'Does she call all the shots?'

'Pretty much!' Father laughed. 'She's a force of nature.'

'Indeed! Well, young lady, what is your third request?' William asked, looking me straight in the eye.

'I think you should build a solar park, like they've got in other parts of Africa. And I think Father should help you to do it.'

I had not seen Father so happy for months. Then he looked a little embarrassed.

'Shall I tell, or will you?' William asked, almost playfully.

'I've been keeping a secret from you, partly because I, too, wanted to see what would happen today before giving my final answer. I have been asked to act as permanent consultant to Jurassic's renewables businesses in the Horn of Africa. Do I accept?'

'Of course!' I said, unable to hide my joy any longer. 'But no more secrets.'

'No more secrets,' Father agreed. 'That goes both ways, though.'

I nodded.

Lucas turned to William. 'It doesn't make sense to call the company Jurassic Oil and Gas anymore, does it? Not if you are really going to do what you say.'

'Once again, you are right on the money. We were thinking of Jurassic Energy. What do you think?'

13 **to call the shots** *(idm)* to have control

'Does what it says on the tin,' said Lucas, adding, 'My dad says that when something's simple and honest.'

'Wise man,' William commented. 'Well, that was easy! Shall we go to lunch?'

5 Lucas wriggled in his seat a bit and then said: 'My great-grandad said burning carbon fuels was like burning sunlight, so if you have a solar park, you'll be working with the sun instead of burning it, won't you?'

William sat back in his chair and closed his eyes.

10 'Not burning sunlight; harnessing it. Hmmm.' He leaned forward and smiled at Lucas. 'I like the sound of that. Can we use it?'

'Yes, of course!' Lucas was absolutely scarlet. 'For a fee!' he added. Everyone burst out laughing.

'You two!' William said, wiping his eyes. 'You two exceptional
15 children give me real hope for our future. You really do and I and my colleagues can never thank you enough. I'll write you a cheque over lunch!'

On the way back, Lucas just couldn't stop staring at that cheque. It was for £500 from William's personal account.

20 'I'll give it to CrisisAid,' he said. 'I shouldn't keep it.'

'Nonsense!' said Father. 'It is your due, you earned it.'

'Maybe I'll save it up so I can visit you in Somaliland, Zaynab,' he said, quietly.

For a moment, my happiness at the day's events evaporated.

25 On the train, we went over and over what had happened in the meeting. It sounded almost too good to be true, but I believed William would do everything he'd said. We'd even persuaded him to get the Exeter office to ask Max's mum if she wanted her job back.

'You did it! You really changed things!' Lucas said, for the zillionth
30 time, his eyes bright, his voice cracked with emotion. 'Your school friends were right, you are their voice. The world is listening to you!'

'No,' I replied, looking into my best ever friend's eager face. 'The world is listening to *us*. Inshallah, it will change.'

---

10 **to harness sth** to control and make use of a natural source of energy – 12 **fee** sum of money that you pay to be allowed to do sth – 14 **exceptional** very special, extraordinary

ZAYNAB

It was over a week since the Jurassic conference and the media frenzy was finally dying down.

It seemed that I had to pay for all the highs by coming down with a thump and I was exhausted again. It was Saturday and pouring rain had stopped me from going out on the moors with Lucas. I huddled on the sofa, wrapped in a blanket with Toffee for company.

Father came to check on me. He had been in a buoyant mood since our London trip, excited about his new role and the prospect of going home, but he seemed extra bouncy as he tugged playfully at the blanket.

'Up you get, lazybones! Have you forgotten that tonight Rafikis are holding a feast in your honour?'

I had forgotten. Father pointed at the clock. 'Come on, my jewel, you need to get ready. I have a surprise for you.'

I looked at him quizzically, but he just smiled and tapped the side of his nose.

'Not telling! You'll just have to be patient!'

I shrugged and went upstairs. As I got dressed, I thought back to that first meal with Lucas. It felt like it was a hundred years ago. Suddenly I noticed a black velvet box on my bed. Inside was a gold chain with an oval locket. I opened it. There was a picture of Mama and Father, smiling and happy. So that was the surprise Father was talking about. It was a lovely one.

I took it downstairs and found Father and Deborah talking in the kitchen.

'Do you like it?' Father said. 'Shall I help you put it on? This locket belonged to your mother's mother and I was to give it to you when

---

1 **media frenzy** *Medienrummel* – 7 **buoyant** ['bɔɪənt] cheerful, happy – 9 **bouncy** lively,
enthusiastic – 12 **feast** large and special meal – 15 **quizzical** questioning, curious –
21 **locket** piece of jewellery, worn around the neck, containing sth such as a picture

you came of age. But I think that day has already arrived and I know Mama would agree.'

He fastened it round my neck and then he held me close.

'Am I forgiven?' he asked, softly.

5   'Yes,' I replied. 'Yes.'

We were the last to arrive at Rafikis, because Bea was late collecting us in the taxi. 'Cattle on the road,' she complained. 'Won't even get out of the way for famous folk like you, Professor, or even you, Zaynab.'

10 Everyone clapped as we walked in. Lucas had saved us places with his family. I had had no idea that they were going to come. I'd never even met Lara.

The café looked and smelled amazing. The Somaliland flag hung across one wall. Cath and the others had printed off pictures of

15 Borama and Hargeisa and laminated them to use as placemats. There were brightly coloured pots with aloes growing in them on every table.

Everyone was smiling and happy and welcoming.

The first course was a deliciously spicy bean stew, very like our

20 maraq digir, with flatbreads and olives.

Father complemented the chef, Caro. 'You made xawaash!' he said. 'Very good. Shukraan jazilaan lak! Thank you so much!'

'Wait until you taste the camel!' she said and then, seeing the look of surprise on his face, 'Yes, we managed to hunt down some

25 camel for you. Not literally, of course.'

'Don't say anything to Dad or Lara. I don't think they heard,' Lucas whispered. 'They'll probably walk out.'

Deborah turned to Father and said in a very low voice, 'Probably not the best moment to tell them you've gone veggie.'

30 Caro had stewed the meat and piled it up on rice and vegetables. Father nodded approvingly. 'Looks good!' he said, scooping up a handful with his fingers, as we would back home.

Lucas and I both turned to check out his family. Lara had her mouth open like a fish.

31 **to scoop up** to lift

'Oh my god,' she said, staring at my father.

'Says the person who sticks her fingers in peanut butter jars!' said Lucas's dad, and he put his knife and fork down and copied my father.

5 'Proper tasty!' he declared. 'Can't beat a bit of venison! But I thought you lot was all starving out there? Going to stop feeling sorry for you, now, if this is your regular nosh!'

The whole restaurant buzzed, but I could not shake off the feeling of melancholy. Lucas, too, was quiet, subdued.

10 'What is it?' I asked.

'You'll be going home soon.'

'Not for two months,' I said, in as cheerful a voice as I could muster.

'Two months. I wanted to show you the moors in spring,' he said, tying his napkin into knots as he spoke.

15 'You could show me via Skype?' I suggested, desperate to cheer us both up.

'Not the same.' He stuck his fork into the delicious honey and orange cake that Cath had just brought to the table.

He was right, it would not be the same.

20 We sat in silence for a moment. We were meant to be celebrating, being happy, being positive, but I felt overwhelmed by sadness.

Suddenly, Father stood up, tapping a teaspoon against his glass to make it ring. 'A few words of thanks, my friends, for this splendid feast, for your very great kindness to me and to Zaynab, for 25 welcoming us into your community. You have made this a home from home and, to be honest, you have given us a problem. Do we stay or do we go back? The board of Jurassic have given me a choice. I can go back to Somaliland and set up the new renewables office there or stay and consult from here. I'll have to go back and forth a 30 bit, which is not ideal, but ...'

So *this* was the surprise, not the locket. I could barely believe my ears, I looked up at him in astonishment.

5 **venison** *Rehfleisch* – 14 **napkin** serviette – 23 **splendid** excellent – 32 **astonishment** surprise

'Zaynab,' he continued, 'I know I should have told you first, but my question is, do we stay?' He addressed the whole café. 'Will you have us?'

'Yes! Stay!' everyone shouted, banging the table with their palms. 'STAY!'

'Zaynab? How do you feel about this?' Father asked.

Lucas looked at me. Stared at me. He spoke very quietly. 'Please. We need you! I know they want you back home, but your voice is loud enough to reach Somaliland from here. You've proved that. Waan ku baryayaa! That means *I beg you*, right? In Somali? I learned it because I wanted to beg you to write to me, but this is so much better. Waan ku baryayaa!'

I felt tears welling up in my eyes. I could feel everyone looking at us.

'Say yes, you daft maid,' Lucas's dad said, through a mouthful of cake. 'He'll be no good to man nor beast if you hop it.'

There was a burst of laughter and I felt as if I might burst, too, but with happiness.

'Yes! Yes! We should stay. We *will* stay,' I said, laughing. 'But you've all got to help. You've all got to do what you can. The campaign doesn't stop. It doesn't stop until we stop the planet from burning sunlight.'

Kitty Harris climbed on the table and started to dance. 'Zaynab's staying! Zaynab's staying!' she sang, spinning wildly and sending cake flying.

I took Lucas's hand and squeezed it hard. 'We've got a lot to do,' I said.

He had the biggest smile on his face. 'I know. But can we start again tomorrow?'

'OK, Ghost Boy. Tomorrow!'

---

13 **to well up** *here:* to fill – 16 **no good to man or beast** *(idm)* completely useless – 16 **to hop it** *(inf)* to leave

Author's note

I chose to have Zaynab come from Somaliland because the country is forecast to be amongst the most badly affected by climate change. We do not pay nearly enough attention to the consequences of waste and consumption on people thousands of miles away or on the disproportionate impact of our actions on women and girls. If we think and act like stewards of all life on this planet, we will care about what is happening to our brothers and sisters the world over and we will do all we can to help.

I am white, educated, privileged. That is an accident of birth. But accidents of birth should not be the determinant of outcomes in life. We have a very long way to go before everyone has equal access to opportunity or, even, to life itself.

CrisisAid is based on the charity, ActionAid, which does invaluable work in the camps in Somaliland, with a particular focus on helping women and girls to be safe, healthy and to have a future.

The words in the word cloud are just some of the words you will need to talk about the topics in *Burning Sunlight*. Use it to start building your own vocabulary. You can also use the vocabulary training tool that you can access with the Klett-Augmented-App (see page 5) – scan this page in the App to revise relevant words and phrases to do with the topics *activism, climate change and relationships*.